MARGINAL MANAGER

MARGINAL MANAGER

The Changing Role of Supervisors in Australia

PETER GILMOUR
RUSSELL D. LANSBURY

University of Queensland Press

First published 1984 by University of Queensland Press
Box 42, St Lucia, Queensland, Australia

Typeset by University of Queensland Press
Printed in Hong Kong by Silex Enterprise & Printing Co.

Distributed in the UK, Europe, the Middle East, Africa, and the
Caribbean by Prentice Hall International, International Book
Distributors Ltd, 66 Wood Lane End, Hemel Hempstead, Herts.,
England

Distributed in the USA and Canada by Technical Impex
Corporation, 5 South Union Street, Lawrence, Mass. 01843 USA

Cataloguing in Publication Data

National Library of Australia

Gilmour, Peter, 1942– .
    The first-line manager and organizational change.

Bibliography.
Includes index.

    1. Organizational change — Australia. 2. Industrial
management — Australia. I. Lansbury, Russell D.
(Russell Duncan), 1945– . II. Title.

658.4′06′0994

ISBN 0 7022 1686 0.

To Caroline and Jock Gilmour,
and Nina and Owen Lansbury

Contents

List of Figures   *ix*

List of Tables   *xi*

Foreword   *xiii*

Preface   *xvii*

PART 1   THE FIRST-LINE MANAGER

1. The Changing Role of the First-Line Manager   *3*
2. The First-Line Manager in Australia: A Survey   *10*
3. Improving the Quality of First-Line Management   *26*

PART 2   MODELS FOR CHANGE

4. The Human Resources Approach   *43*
   Case 1: The Lakewood Plant   *52*
   Case 2: The Elizabeth Plant   *59*
5. The Grid Organization Development Approach   *64*
   Case 3: Mount Newman Mining Company   *69*
6. The Group Technology Approach   *80*
   Case 4: Mulgrave Gear   *89*
   Case 5: Ajax Pumps   *92*
7. The Socio-Technical Systems Approach   *95*
   Case 6: The Kalmar Assembly Plant   *105*
   Case 7: Woodlawn Mines   *114*
   Case 8: Siddons Industries   *125*

PART 3   CONCLUSIONS

8. Prospects for the First-Line Manager and Organizational
    Change   *133*

Notes   *158*
Bibliography   *164*
Index   *177*

Figures

1. Types of supervisory systems   6
2. The vicious circle of the supervisor's role   9
3. Cluster analysis showing important characteristics of the supervisor's role   16
4. Interlinking perspectives of the supervisor's role in terms of important characteristics   17
5. Types of organizational situation, corresponding to task structure   28
6. Evaluating the effects of supervision, according to different situations   29
7. Profile of organizational characteristics   44
8. Interlocking work groups   47
9. Vertical and lateral interlocking groups in a Brisbane hospital   49
10. Vertical interlocking groups in a retail organization   50
11. Changes in the operating efficiency of the Lakewood plant   56
12. An analysis of problems at the Elizabeth plant   60
13. The Managerial Grid   65
14. The organization development programme of Mount Newman Mining Company   75
15. Functional plant layout   81
16. Group plant layout   82
17. Flow-line plant layout   83
18. The organization as an open system   96

19. The traditional structure of work organization in the production section of a factory   99
20. The structure of a semi-autonomous work team in the production section of a factory   100
21. The assembly process at the Volvo plant in Kalmar, Sweden   107
22. Organizational structure of engineering operations at Woodlawn Mines compared with a traditional mining company   117
23. The training programme at Woodlawn   120
24. The management system at Woodlawn   122
25. The organization structure at Siddons Industries   127
26. Manufacturing process flow   128
27. The effects of corporate strategy on first-line management   144
28. The workshop programme   152
29. A diagnostic model for organizational change   154

Tables

1. Characteristics of the supervisor's role rated in terms of importance   15
2. Aspects of supervisory style rated in terms of importance   20
3. Supervisory style and personal characteristics of respondents   21
4. Expected future career paths   23
5. Career orientations and personal characteristics of supervisors   24
6. Basic personal traits of supervisors   27
7. Type of supervisory training and frequency of use   35
8. Summary of man-days lost in the Pilbara owing to industrial disputes   73
9. Typical job design: group technology and traditional batch manufacture   84
10. Features of group technology manufacture   88
11. Operating areas at Woodlawn   119
12. The impact of production systems on aspects of work organization   139
13. Organizational characteristics and orientations of first-line management   142
14. The normative effect of the type of production process on first-line management   146

Foreword

"The first-line supervisor is the critical link in the managerial chain." Though this statement is almost a truism, first-line supervisors are typically ignored by managers and academic researchers alike. Instead, attention is focused on higher managers or on rank-and-file workers. After all, higher managers deal with larger, more glamorous issues; further, top executives are more familiar with their problems. By contrast, rank-and-file employees have the ability to voice their grievances through their union and through industrial action.

Since the first-level supervisor occupies the lowest level of managerial jobs, it is commonly assumed that this job must also be the simplest. Allegedly, all he or she need do is make sure that top management's instructions are carried out. But in fact foremen are required to fill at least three roles: (1) supervising their subordinates, (2) dealing with higher management and other departments (sometimes called the linking pin function), and (3) resolving technical problems. None of these roles has ever been simple, and over time the nature of supervisors' jobs has become increasingly complex and diverse. The simple assumption that all such jobs are the same is no longer true today, especially as technology has advanced so quickly. Supervisory work has changed much more rapidly than most observers have been aware. Unfortunately, the assumption that supervisors' tasks are easy had led typically to their being denied the tools (especially the status, authority, and training) required to do their job.

Supervisors today face most of the problems of higher management plus some special problems of their own. From company chairman to first-line supervisor, orders flow downward in a reasonably effective manner. Generally, each level obeys the instructions of those above. Outright resistance is rare. With some justification it is assumed that all levels of management are motivated by organizational loyalty. But the foreman-worker relationship is far different from relationships at higher levels. Rank-and-file workers can and do resist orders that they think are unfair. The pressure that the foreman gets from above is hard to pass down below.

It was not always so. The supervisor's job has been constantly changing. At the dawn of the industrial revolution foremen had tremendous discretion. At least in the United States, they had the power to hire, to fire (for any reason or none), to determine work methods, and occasionally to set pay. Their main methods of motivation were threats and fear. Workers were completely dependent on them and opportunities for arbitrariness and tyranny were rife.

The traditional role of the foreman persists in many unskilled jobs and especially with new immigrants (whether in Australia or the United States); however, with the advent of unions the traditional approach was largely replaced by human relations. Many of the foreman's old powers, especially those of hiring (and often of firing), were given to higher management or the personnel department. Foremen were expected to be "fair but firm", to get to know their subordinates as people, and to provide a friendly, supportive atmosphere in which to work. Meanwhile work methods were frequently determined by the industrial engineering department. This made sense on simple jobs and with poorly educated workers. Workers felt that they had "a good place to work" and in return they typically put in "a fair day's work", their stint, but not much more.

Better educated workers today are increasingly asking for jobs that are challenging, meaningful, and offer opportunities for discretion. Newer technologies, especially the use of computers and robots, as well as other forms of "high tech", are requiring concomitant changes in work structures and worker attitudes. The compliant obedience engendered by human relations is not enough. Instead, the new ways of work require entirely new relationships between first-line managers and their subordinates. This is especially the case in companies engaging in the various forms of job redesign, group technology, and quality of work life experiments that the authors describe. All these vastly change the first-line manager's job. He or she becomes more of a coordinator, facilitator and resource person (expert) than a boss. The main job is now to provide advice and win consensus rather than to give orders. A greater portion of time is spent serving as a linking pin with other departments and higher management.

Making changes of this sort is never easy and is unlikely to occur without careful planning. Indeed, as the authors argue, management needs to give much more explicit thought to the roles it expects the first-line supervisor to play, even where technology has not changed. To facilitate this task of reevaluating the supervisor's role, the book offers a succint summary of the major research work and theoretical approaches relevant to first-line management. It argues that supervisors differ and should differ in their behaviour from one situation to another, depending on such factors as the nature of the work, the size of the company, and the skills and attitudes of the workers involved. It presents some new Australian evidence as to the career paths of first-line managers and how they view their jobs, making the valuable distinction between two kinds of foreman: supervisors who start as rank-and-file workers and see the foreman's job as the culmination of their career, and better educated managers who start their careers as foremen but expect to be promoted rapidly into higher management. Then, having analyzed both foremen and their jobs, it examines the foreman training process, emphasizing the need to start each training programme with an analysis of the nature of the managerial job in the given instance.

Finally, the book reports on recent Australian and other quality of work life and job design experiments. Much of this is new to the non-Australian reader.

George Strauss
Professor of Industrial Relations and Management
University of California, Berkeley.

Preface

Considerable change has occurred during recent years in the role of the marginal manager — the supervisor or first-line manager — within industry. This book examines these changes in the context of the Australian workplace and discusses the likely role the first-line manager will play in the future.

Much of the book is based on information generated during two research projects funded by the Technical and Further Education (TAFE) Council of the Tertiary Education Commission. The first project involved a large-scale survey of supervisors, most of whom were engaged in supervision courses at the time. In the second project, a number of detailed case studies were undertaken of first-line managers in various organizational settings. We would like to thank Beth Moran and Gary Hilton of the Technical and Further Education Council for their support and encouragement during these projects and the organizations that permitted us to collect our case studies. The Directors of Technical and Further Education in each state, and their organizations, were also very supportive and helpful in providing facilities essential for the successful completion of the project.

The most important people in the preparation of this book were the first-line managers. Although many of the subjects of the research were probably bemused by the process of academic interrogation to which they were subjected, they were most helpful and often eloquent in describing the work they did. Particular thanks are due to the following: Teddy

Papazoglou, George Cotton, Jack Collins, Bob McLean, Nada Sismanovic, Max McGinnis, Bob Eggleston, Jack Smith, Barrie Dempster, Peter Malcolm, Gordon Jackson, Bill Ingles, John Burgess, Arthur Dell, Clem Morris, Bevan Lennie, and Robert Hawkes. We also appreciated the opportunity to discuss with John Siddons his ideas on industrial democracy.

Stephanie Phillips worked with us as a research assistant on the first TAFE project. She carried out the large information-processing task with considerable effectiveness. Bianca Golotta, Ruth O'Ryan, Pauline Casey, and Neddy Campbell at Monash, and Elizabeth Polgar, Margaret Knowlden, and Elizabeth Tracy at Macquarie provided fast and reliable secretarial services during the five years we spent on this work.

Peter Gilmour
Russell D. Lansbury

PART 1

THE FIRST-LINE MANAGER

1

The Changing Role of the First-Line Manager

First-line management is the lubricant that enables organizations to put into operation at the workplace the directives of management. But despite the key role played by many first-line managers or supervisors, their organizational contribution has often been ignored. For most supervisors in Australia the position represents the culmination of a career as a worker on the "shop floor"; but the position often requires severance from former workmates and resignation from the union, while not providing complete acceptance into management ranks. Recent interest in first-line management has resulted mainly from dissatisfaction with the traditional supervisory role and suggestions for either strengthening the position or replacing it with other concepts, such as autonomous work groups. Should the position be abolished or enhanced? Is the first-line manager to become more or less important in the future? Should organizations attempt to develop work structures that can operate effectively without a supervisor, or should organizations ensure that the first-line manager or supervisor is provided with training and other resources so that the job can be performed with maximum efficiency and competence?

Identifying and Defining the First-Line Manager

Although the first-line manager or supervisor is widely recognized as occupying an important position within work organizations, there are many different meanings attached to the term *supervision*. Thurley and Wirdenius identify three ways in which supervisors may be distinguished from other employees: by their job titles, by the managerial status and authority accorded to them, and by the tasks they carry out.[1] Job titles are probably the least satisfactory method of defining a supervisor. Some titles such as *foreman, leading hand*, or *supervisor* are used in a specific way in particular organizations. Furthermore, a survey by the National Institute of Industrial Psychology in Britain[2] identified more than two hundred titles among men and women regarded as supervisors. Similarly, a study by the Swedish Council for Personnel Administration[3] reported at least a dozen possible translations of the title *supervisor* into Swedish. It is important to note that the term *supervisor* is a general organizational title, while *foreman* is an occupational title. The increased usage of the former in preference to the latter probably indicates a decline in trade consciousness among supervisors, though not necessarily the emergence of a new "supervisor" consciousness.[4] For the sake of simplicity, and in line with practical usage, the terms *first-line manager* and *supervisor* are used interchangeably in this book.

A second method of defining supervision is by reference to the supervisor's status and authority. One such example appeared in a British government publication on supervision: "A supervisor is a person in constant control of a definite section of a labour force in an undertaking, exercising it either directly or through subordinates and responsible for this to higher management."[5]

While supervisors are formally recognized as having some degree of authority over others, it has often been noted that they occupy a marginal position between management and the workers. Numerous studies have argued that the supervisors feel like "people in the middle" and desire greater status and authority to equalize their responsibilities and authority.[6] In recent years, an increasing proportion of supervisors in various countries have formed or joined unions because they feel neglected or ignored by management and lack authority in the workplace. One contributing factor, according to Grabe and Silberer,[7] is that supervisors tend to be given work left over by managers and specialists. They are expected to correct the errors of others so that the work group will not suffer.

A third method of defining supervision is in terms of a number of common "supervisory tasks". Studies of jobs performed by supervisors, however, show that these tend to vary with the level of supervision and according to the industry concerned. A supervisor's job may include such things as clerical work, inspection of raw materials, instruction to operatives, repairing machines, and settling disputes with shop stewards. While it is difficult, if not impossible, to accurately assess the average amount of time devoted by a supervisor to any of these tasks, studies have shown that "people mangement" or "leadership" tasks comprise a fairly small proportion of the total.[8] In the words of Thurley and Wirdenius, "a supervisor's job appears to be an empty box, to be filled with activities and tasks according to the particular situation".[9]

The most satisfactory way of defining supervision is probably in terms of the supervisor's work role. According to George Strauss,[10] there are at least three basic supervisory roles. Firstly, there is a "pure" type of supervisory role, in which the supervisor has direct control over a production system and is clearly recognized as such. Secondly, there is a mixed type of supervisory/managerial role, where the supervisor is concerned with specialized tasks but does not have control over a production system. Thirdly, there is a mixed type of supervisor/worker role, where an individual has formal status as a supervisor but not the actual authority in practice. Examples of the first type of supervisory role include the traditional craft foreman as well as the production supervisor on a car assembly line. The second type of supervisory role is illustrated by technical specialists who have supervisory status but do not actually supervise staff. The third type is represented by process operators who help to control the production system but do not see themselves as supervisors. The main point that emerges from this analysis is that it is difficult to distinguish the exact boundaries of the supervisor's role.

The interaction of different types of supervisory roles creates systems of supervision. In large or complex organizations, the

supervisory system may consist of four or more levels of
people who are regarded as carrying out supervisory roles. The
various levels may be called by titles such as leading hand,
instructor, junior foreman, senior foreman, and shift supervisor.

As shown in figure 1, Thurley and Wirdenius classify different supervisory systems according to two dimensions: (1) the
degree of autonomy that supervisors have in their work situation, and their freedom from management control; and (2) the

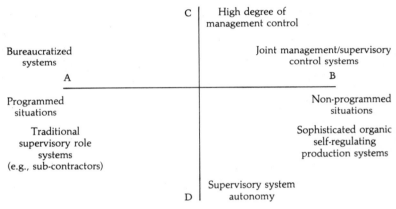

Source: Thurley and Wirdenius, *Supervision,* p. 29.

Figure 1   Types of supervisory systems

degree to which supervisory situations and tasks are programmed. This type of classification yields four different supervisory systems: a traditional system, where the supervisor has a
high degree of autonomy but within programmed situations; a
bureaucratic system, where there is a high degree of management control and programmed situations; a joint
management/supervisory system, where non-programmed
situations are combined with a high degree of management control; and an organic, self-regulating system, where a high degree
of supervisory autonomy is combined with non-programmed
situations.

The Changing Role of the First-Line Manager

The role of the first-line manager was formalized at a very early stage of industrialization and has been slow to change. Numerous historians have traced the gradual metamorphosis of the master craftsmen into a craft foreman, or *Meister*, role.[11] Early factories in England advertised for craftsmen in certain trades in order to develop them into engineers and foremen. Not surprisingly, the master craftsmen carried their personal social status with them in their new supervisory roles. This was aided, in England, by the lack of any theory or concept of large-scale organization.[12] During this formative period, the foreman controlled recruitment and dismissals, as well as discipline and the type of bonus and remuneration, and dealt with grievances and complaints. A statement made by construction employers to the Charity Organization Society in 1880 clearly demonstrates the significance of the foreman's role: "You trust the foreman to find your men and he generally finds those he knows and they would be those in the district that he lives in. . . . The foreman in each trade is held partially responsible, not only for the number of men but for the quality."[13]

The twentieth century has witnessed the gradual decline in the status of the supervisor and a diminution of the supervisor's role. The development of larger and more complex organizations created the need for staff departments, which in turn eroded the authority of the supervisor. This development is aptly illustrated by the emergence of the personnel function, which took over aspects of recruitment, selection, training, remuneration, and industrial relations from the supervisor.[14] Other staff departments responsible for work study, quality control, and planning have also encroached upon the supervisor's role. The increase in the number of technologists and graduates entering the ranks of middle and senior management has also reduced the career opportunities and promotion prospects for supervisors. Technological changes, such as the introduction of computers to improve production processes and planning, have also affected the supervisor's role.[15] According to Daniel Nelson, the technicians and staff specialists who

dominate the present-day manufacturing plant have significantly eroded "the foreman's empire".[16]

The Future of First-Line Management

During the past few decades, first-line management has
undergone changes as a result of social, economic, and
technological trends. Included among these trends are automa-
tion, rationalization and specialization, the widening of labour
markets and the collapse of wage differentials, demands for
greater equality in the workplace, participation by employees
in the decision-making process, dependence by enterprises on
government planning, and the prevalence of feelings of anxiety
and stress among supervisors. Thurley and Wirdenius identify
four possible alternatives that may occur in the future:

1. Supervision will wither away and be replaced by a more "democratic"
   economic order in which workers and operatives will be relatively
   autonomous.
2. Supervision will lose its specific and recognizable characteristics and be
   replaced by work organizations which are bureaucratic in structure
   throughout.
3. Supervision will be "professionalized", forming an occupation with
   specific tasks which is recognized as competent to regulate its own
   affairs.
4. Supervision will be transformed into temporary problem-solving teams
   which will preserve their "production" functions, but not the status of
   the members of the team.[17]

Although some groups of supervisors have aspired to "professionalization", they have generally been in a weak power
position. The main trend, therefore, has been towards the pro-
gressive unionization of supervisors and the development of a
more formalized industrial relations system regulating levels
and content of jobs. It is important to note that the system of
conciliation and arbitration in Australia has meant that industrial relations is already highly formalized. However, supervisors have not been as highly unionized in Australia as they
are in some other countries.[18] A second trend has been
increased bureaucratization, which has limited the degree of
discretion available to supervisors in the performance of their

work. As shown in figure 2, this has led to a vicious circle of declining flexibility and adaptability in work organizations, allied to low job satisfaction, little role identification, and growing demarcation problems between blue- and white-collar unions.

Thurley and Wirdenius argue that supervision needs to be reappraised, reformulated, and redeveloped, because it has been conceptualized in ways that are highly misleading. The various perceptions of the "problem" of supervision, they argue, reflect the emerging crisis of supervision. Accordingly, they advocate the development of a system of "process evaluation" designed to measure successful approaches to supervisory development, and to demonstrate that supervision is not a forgotten area.[19]

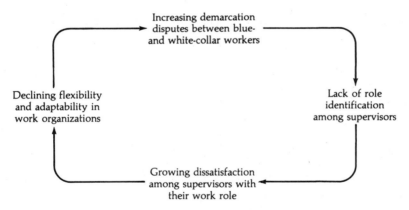

Figure 2   The vicious circle of the supervisor's role

2

The First-Line Manager in Australia: A Survey

The role of the first-line manager has long been regarded as a "problem area" of industrial relations. At a seminar on "Sources of Worker Dissatisfaction in Australia", a personnel manager from ICI Australia cited "the poor quality of supervision" as a major cause of industrial unrest: "The climate . . . set by supervisors enforcing close controls [leads] to the non-involvement of people in their job."[1] An organizer with the Vehicle Builders Employees Federation, also speaking at that seminar, claimed that "greater attention by employers to more effective and efficient training of supervisory personnel . . . is one of the most essential steps to be taken in overcoming worker dissatisfaction".[2] Thurley and Wirdenius note that the complaints about supervisors are remarkably similar in different countries: "It is stated that unless management tries to modify supervisory attitudes and change supervisory practices, it will be impossible to carry out any effective modification in industry."[3] In recent times, advocates of job design, autonomous work groups, and other new forms of work organization have urged the abolition of the supervisor or at least a radical restructuring of the supervisor's role.[4]

A sociological view of the supervisor's role has generally been expressed in terms of "ambiguity" or "marginality". The supervisor has been variously described as "the man in the middle",[5] "a master and victim of double talk",[6] and a "marginal man".[7] These labels arise mainly from the supervisor's position in the hierarchy of command, which is somewhere between the management and the worker, and therefore in the middle and at the margin of both. Ambiguity in turn increases stress, or role strain, for the supervisor. E.V. Schneider suggests that the strain in the supervisor's role may be attributed to two main sources.[8] First, the supervisor has been progressively displaced by newer specialist groups, such as personnel managers and industrial engineers, who have taken over various aspects of the job.[9] Second, there has been a general decline in the salary and status of the supervisor relative to both management and workers. This has been hastened by the professionalization of management and the growth of unionization among white-collar and other hitherto less organized groups.[10]

Another factor contributing to the "marginality" of the supervisor is that the role was formalized at a very early stage in the process of industrial development and has been slow to change. In Western Europe, according to Thurley and Wirdenius, supervisors traditionally learned their role behaviour directly from other supervisors rather than from the managers or entrepreneurs in organizations for which they worked.[11] This has led to a situation where the supervisors have gradually become socially and technically out of date, and parts of their role have been taken over by others. A number of general criticisms have been made against the supervisor in contemporary organizations. They include resistance to change and defence of the status quo, inability to solve problems systematically, lack of knowledge about modern technology, inadequate appreciation of industrial relations matters, and poor human relation skills. The shortcomings of the supervisor, it is argued, have led to problems such as high labour turnover, absenteeism, low job satisfaction, inadequate planning, and the inability to meet work schedules.[12]

There are conflicting views about the future shape of the supervisor's role. Despite the apparent loss of power, status, and authority, the supervisor remains a significant figure not only in the factory but also in the office. According to Dunkerley, "the supervisor's role loses nothing of its complexity, even if the influences making for this role are different from those which applied before".[13] Nevertheless, the supervisor is in a period of transition. Two alternative trends which may affect the future role of the supervisor are (*a*) the movement for greater democratization of the workplace and (*b*) the development of more centralized management control systems. In the past, top management has tended to allow supervisors considerable autonomy at the workplace level. However, much of the emphasis in schemes of industrial democracy and other organizational changes has been upon giving employees more control over the organization of their work. In such circumstances, the supervisor is expected to become more integrated with the work group and be less of an overseer.[14] Nevertheless, the increasing size and complexity of organizations has also led to the growth of centralized control systems and a consequent diminution of the supervisor's autonomy. (This is especially relevant in cases where computerized management information systems are introduced into an organization.) Hence, the supervisor is faced with the need to adapt to rapidly changing circumstances.

The emergence of industrial democracy or worker participation in management as an issue of increasing importance has coincided with a revival of interest in the role of the first-line manager or supervisor. The introduction of semi-autonomous work groups, as a means of giving workers more direct say in the organization of their work, has been viewed by some as a threat to the future existence of the supervisor. T.U. Qvale, however, argues that the role of the supervisor will be expanded by these changes; instead of being the "man in the middle" the supervisor will have a new role as a "boundary regulator" between autonomous production units, managers, and staff experts.[15] Whether or not these predictions are fulfilled, it is clear that the role of the supervisor is changing.[16]

Background to the Study

In 1975 a study was commissioned by the Technical and Further Education Commission (now incorporated within the Tertiary Education Commission) to examine supervisory-level education in Australia, with special reference to the courses offered by Technical and Further Education (TAFE) institutes.[17] In its submission to the Inquiry into Technical and Further Education in Australia (the Kangan Committee) in 1973,[18] the Commonwealth Department of Labour (as it was called then) noted that there existed "a vast gap between the training provided for supervisors and post-graduate education". The department argued that there was a need for systematic development of technically oriented supervisory and first-line management education and training, which could be undertaken by those without prior formal qualifications. The curriculum, it argued, should be broadly based and include such fields as management methods, industrial relations, and social change and community values. In its subsequent report,[19] the Kangan Committee argued that TAFE institutes should expand their activities in the field of supervisory-level education for both private and public sectors. TAFE could make a positive contribution by developing specialist teachers in this field.

The study was therefore designed to investigate the nature of courses in supervision and first-line management offered at TAFE institutes throughout Australia and to recommend future programmes and policies in this field. The research also sought to ascertain the attitudes of students undertaking these courses in order to draw some conclusions about the relevance of TAFE courses to the needs of supervisors.

The research strategy employed in the study was based on a series of postal questionnaires, supplemented by interviews, with the following respondents: students undertaking supervision courses at TAFE institutes (a sub-sample of whom were sent follow-up questionnaires one year after they had completed their course); supervisors who had not attended any TAFE courses; lecturers in supervision at TAFE institutes; employers of supervisory staff; and trade union officials in whose organizations supervisors were represented. Visits were also made to each state to observe supervision courses at TAFE institutes and to interview administrators, lecturers, and students involved in supervision education. The results reported in this chapter are based mainly upon data obtained from twelve hundred respondents enrolled in the Certificate of

Supervision at TAFE institutes in 1975. This sample represented a response rate of approximately 80 per cent.

Who Is the First-Line Manager?

The twelve hundred respondents undertaking TAFE supervision courses were drawn from a wide range of backgrounds. It is therefore useful to provide a profile of the sample.

The average age of the supervisors in the study was thirty-two years. There appeared, however, to be three main groups: "young" supervisors under twenty-four years constituted almost one-quarter of the total sample; an "intermediate" group, aged between twenty-five and thirty-nine years, made up a little more than half of the total; and an "older" group, over the age of forty years, formed the remaining twenty-five per cent.

Almost half of the respondents had completed an apprenticeship or the equivalent before becoming a supervisor, one-fifth had completed high school, and the remainder had left school earlier. Approximately one-third, therefore, could be classified as having minimal formal qualifications. Before their present job, one-third of the respondents had worked in a skilled trade, one-fifth had been in a clerical or sales position, and about one-quarter were in semi-skilled or unskilled work. Hence, three broad groups could be discerned on the basis of their background: white-collar workers, skilled tradesmen, and semi-skilled or unskilled workers. A further distinction should be drawn between two-thirds of the sample who currently held supervisory level positions and one-third who were working in other jobs at the time of the survey.

Only 6 per cent of respondents were women and less than 4 per cent were born in non-English-speaking countries. Thus, women and non-British migrants were under-represented in the study, although this was not due to the sampling procedures used. While 60 per cent of respondents were the children of blue-collar workers, almost 25 per cent had fathers who had been in supervisory or similar positions. Thus, while there was considerable inter-generational mobility, many supervisors had followed their fathers into the same field.

Perception of the Role of the First-Line Manager

Respondents were asked to rate a list of twenty-two characteristics, describing aspects of the supervisor's role, on a seven-point scale from "not important" to "very important". The characteristics, which are shown in table 1, were derived from open-ended interviews with a sub-sample of respondents.

Table 1 Characteristics of the supervisor's role rated in terms of importance (in percentages)

Characteristic	Not Important		Moderately Important			Very Important		Average Ranking
	1	2	3	4	5	6	7	
A pleasant personality	0	0	1	11	18	25	43	6.0
An ability to effectively communicate with subordinates	0	0	0	1	2	13	83	6.8
An interest in safety	0	0	1	6	10	22	59	6.4
A recognition of human needs in the work place	0	0	0	6	14	24	54	6.3
An ability to counsel subordinates	0	0	1	8	16	25	47	6.1
Commonsense	0	0	0	2	6	17	73	6.6
An ability to train subordinates	0	0	1	7	13	23	53	6.2
A company orientation	1	1	3	21	23	21	26	5.4
High technical skills in his/her trade	1	1	3	18	21	23	31	5.6
Conscientiousness	0	0	0	6	12	29	49	6.3
An ability to motivate subordinates	0	0	1	2	5	26	64	6.7
An effective leader	0	0	0	2	6	22	69	6.6
Patience	0	0	1	7	15	24	51	6.1
An ability to help subordinates	0	0	0	4	10	31	53	6.4
Honesty	0	0	0	4	5	14	75	6.6
Reliability	0	0	0	1	4	18	75	6.7
Sound judgment	0	0	0	4	9	27	59	6.4
Being willing to change	0	0	1	8	12	26	51	6.2
Trusworthiness	0	0	0	2	6	18	72	6.6
An ability to make decisions	0	0	0	1	3	17	76	6.7
Easygoing	10	6	12	30	20	9	13	4.2
An ability to communicate with management	0	0	1	3	4	22	69	6.6

Although most respondents regarded all the characteristics as important, some differences emerged with regard to the degree of importance they attached to each characteristic. In order to further explore these differences, cluster analysis was carried out. This revealed two broad clusters of characteristics.[20] As shown in figure 3, the first cluster comprised characteristics related mainly to the technical nature of the job, such as decision-making ability, sound judgement, reliability, an

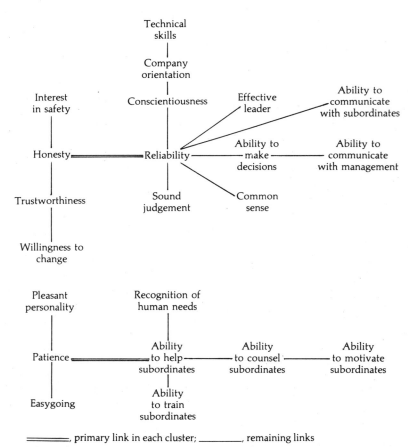

Figure 3   Cluster analysis showing important characteristics of the supervisor's role

interest in safety, and technical skills. The second cluster, by contrast, related more to social aspects of the job, such as patience, helpfulness, counselling skills, and the ability to motivate others. The "technical skills" cluster was rated more highly than the cluster relating to "social skills". This confirmed other findings reported in the literature, that supervisors tend to pay less attention to the "human relations" aspects of their roles and to rely more heavily on technical skills often acquired in their previous occupation.[21]

Respondents were also required to comment on what they regarded as their employer's expectations of their role behaviour. They were invited to list the three most important qualities that an effective supervisor should possess. Then they were asked which qualities they thought their employer would consider a good supervisor should have. The characteristics most commonly mentioned by a sub-sample of fifty respondents are shown in figure 4. It is interesting to note that there was agreement on only four main characteristics: decision-making ability, communication with subordinates, ef-

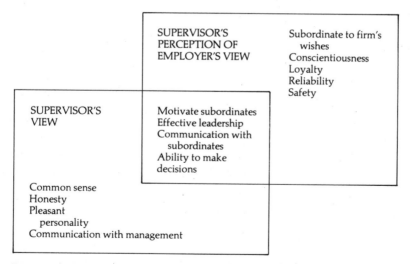

Figure 4   Interlinking perspectives of the supervisor's role in terms of important characteristics

fective leadership, and the ability to motivate subordinates. Supervisors tended to perceive their employers as assigning greater importance to their "technical expertise". One interesting implication of these results is that they may explain the tendency of supervisors to underplay the importance of the "human relations" or "people-related" aspects of their role because they perceive that their superiors expect them to pay more regard to "technical" considerations. This may also be the source of potential misunderstanding between senior management and supervisors.

Supervisory Styles

Much has been written about supervisory styles and behaviour. Early research by proponents of the "human relations" approach highlighted the importance of informal groups within organizations and the need for supervisors to secure the commitment of these groups to organizational goals.[22] Following in this tradition, Lewin, Lippitt, and White[23] introduced the concept of an "authoritarian-democratic-laissez faire" continuum, based on the degree of subordinate participation in decision-making. This rather simplistic classification suggested that the authoritarian supervisor was interested primarily in production, and the democratic supervisor primarily in people. In a similar vein, Likert[24] compared employee-centred and job-centred supervisory styles and reported that the former generally led to higher levels of production and greater employee satisfaction. McGregor[25] introduced the concepts of Theory X and Theory Y (see chap. 4) to explain the assumptions about human behaviour upon which supervisory or managerial actions are based. Theory Y assumes, among other things, that individuals will exercise self-direction and self-control under appropriate conditions and will therefore require less formal supervision. Although the human-relations school has been strongly criticized on the grounds of its inbuilt conservative bias, lack of empirical rigour, and failure to address the issue of conflict, it has nevertheless had important implications for the development of certain supervisory styles.

In the study, some of the concepts underlying Theory X and Theory Y, applied to supervisory practices, were operational-ized. Respondents were asked to rate ten statements about supervisory styles on a seven-point scale, from "strongly disagree" to "strongly agree". These statements did not necessarily reflect the way in which supervisors actually behave, but they indicated something of their underlying assumptions concerning appropriate supervisory styles. For simplicity, each statement was designated *a priori* as reflecting support for the Theory X or Theory Y assumptions about super-visory style. Table 2 lists the statements, the frequency of responses, and average ratings. The findings indicate general support among the respondents for Theory X assumptions con-cerning appropriate supervisory styles.

In order to test whether any major differences existed between supervisors favouring either Theory X or Theory Y assumptions, the total respondents were divided into two groups based upon their individual scores on the questions dealing with supervisory styles. As shown in table 3, dif-ferences in the mean value of a range of characteristics for the two groups were significant only in a few cases. The respondents who favoured Theory Y assumptions tended to be older, in a less senior position, worked for smaller organiza-tions, and supervised a large number of subordinates.

It is important to acknowledge that McGregor's dual theory of supervisory styles is rather simplistic and is not intended to be applied literally to every situation. The effectiveness of any particular style of supervision will depend on a variety of factors, including the amount of formal or informal power of the supervisor within an organization and the type or purpose of the organization. In a voluntary type of organization, for example, the supervisor's ability to obtain the loyalty of the members will be of crucial importance. In a production organization he may be able to rely on other means to attain his objectives, such as financial incentives or the threat of dismissal. Fiedler[26] has introduced a "contingency model" which states that the appropriate supervisory style in a given situation is a function of leader-member relations, task structure, and posi-

Table 2 Aspects of supervisory style rated in terms of importance (in percentages)

Statement	Strongly Disagree			Undecided			Strong Agree		Average Ranking
	1	2	3	4	5	6	7		
Staff should be closely supervised in order to get better work for them.	14	12	13	10	18	15	10		3.0
The supervisor should set goals and objectives for his/her staff and sell them on the merits of his plan.	4	2	5	10	15	27	30		1.5
The supervisor should set up controls to ensure that his/her staff are getting the job done.	2	2	4	6	17	32	30		1.3
The supervisor should encourage his/her staff to set their own goals and objectives.	5	3	5	8	12	26	33		5.5
The supervisor should make sure his/her staff's work is planned out for them.	2	2	5	8	14	25	36		1.3
The supervisor should check with his/her staff daily to see if they need any help.	2	1	2	2	8	25	52		0.8
The supervisor should step in as soon as reports indicate that the job is slipping.	1	1	2	4	10	26	46		1.0
Staff should be pushed to meet schedules if necessary.	11	6	9	13	20	20	12		2.5
The supervisor should have frequent meetings with his/her staff to keep in touch with what is going on.	1	1	1	4	9	21	54		0.7
Staff should be allowed to make important decisions.	16	7	9	15	19	16	41		4.1

Table 3 Supervisory style and personal characteristics of respondents (Average responses)

| Personal Characteristics | Supervisory Style Favoured | | Total Average |
	Theory X (n = 540)	Theory Y (n = 564)	(n = 1,104)
Age	30.90	32.20*	31.40
Father's occupational status†	4.46	4.50	4.48
Father's educational level‡	3.39	3.47	3.43
Own occupational status†	3.64	3.50	3.56
Own educational level‡	3.94	3.79	3.87
Number of subordinates	5.40	7.50*	6.50
Size of organization	283	262	272

* Significant above the 1 per cent level of confidence ($p < 0.01$)
† Where
1 = Professional and top managerial
2 = Para-professional and lower managerial
3 = Supervisory and self-employed
4 = Clerical and sales
5 = Skilled
6 = Semi-skilled
7 = Unskilled
‡ Where
1 = Some primary school
2 = Completed primary school
3 = Some secondary school
4 = Completed secondary school
5 = Some technical college
6 = Completed technical college

tion power. The combination of these variables determines the "favourableness of the situation" for a particular supervisory style.

Career Orientations of First-Line Managers

Another aspect selected for investigation in the study concerned the career orientations of supervisors. Previous studies have indicated that differences in career history and aspirations often have an important influence on the way in which individuals approach their job. According to Sofer,[27] a career is conceived in both "prospect" and "retrospect" or, in other words, is viewed in terms of both the past and the future. Most employees tend to define their career aspirations in terms of expectations about the opportunities available within or outside their current organization. Most employing organizations, however, have only a limited number of higher-level posts available, and individuals must therefore adjust their ambitions to fit the situation or seek promotion elsewhere. In an early study of career orientations, Gouldner[28] used the categories "cosmopolitan" and "local" to discriminate between the attitudes of teaching staff in an American university. "Cosmopolitans" were characterized by strong commitment to a career based on specialized role skills, the use of an external or professional reference group, and a low degree of loyalty to their employing organization. "Locals", on the other hand, felt a primary loyalty to their employing organization, lacked a sense of commitment to their specialism, and used an internal or organizational reference group.

Numerous studies have subsequently been conducted among various occupational groups which used these and other typologies. In general, it has been found that career orientations tend to have a powerful influence on the behaviour of individuals within organizations. In a study of technical specialists,[29] Lansbury identified three predominant career orientations which he labelled "functionary", "academic", and "careerist". These orientations were found to have considerable significance for the development of work roles among technical specialists. A similar conclusion was drawn by Rapoport[30] from a study of mid-career managers. "Whilst it is well known", argued Rapoport, "that men may pursue organizational careers through various functional channels such as finance, personnel, production and so on, it is less well understood how differences in orientation to an employing organization can yield contrasting styles or strategies which cut across occupational groups." Accordingly, the study sought to illuminate the dynamics of career orientations among supervisors and its interrelationship with various background variables.

Three broad career paths were conceptualized as available to supervisors: movement into a higher managerial position within their current organization, movement into a completely different field of work within their current organization, and

movement into another organization within the same or different occupation. As shown in table 4, six options were
presented to respondents, which included various combinations
of the above career paths. The second and fourth explicitly indicated that respondents aspired to move to a higher managerial
position either within or outside their current organization.
Respondents were classified as having a "managerial" career
orientation if their average ratings on the second and fourth
options were greater than 5 on a seven-point scale from "not
likely" to "very likely". A "supervisory" career orientation was
established if respondents' average ratings on these questions
were less than 3.

Table 4   Expected future career paths
(in percentages)

Career Path	Not Likely	Quite Likely	Very Likely
Stay with my present employer in my current position	35.5	37.2	27.3
Stay with my present employer in a higher position in the same area of work	16.8	42.0	41.2
Stay with my present employer in a different area of work	46.0	37.0	17.0
Transfer to another organization in a higher position in the same area of work	53.7	31.8	14.5
Transfer to another organization in the same position in the same area of work	76.5	19.2	4.3
Transfer to another organization in a different area of work	69.7	22.4	7.9

Note: This question was answered on a seven-point scale. Responses 1 and 2 have been
combined as "not likely", 3, 4, and 5 as "quite likely", and 6 and 7 as "very likely".

In order to establish likely correlates of these two broad
career orientations, respondents were divided into two groups
labelled "managerial" and "supervisory" and compared on a
number of variables including age, educational level, previous
career history, number of people currently supervised, size of
employing organization, and the educational and occupational
background of their fathers. As shown in table 5, those

Table 5   Career orientations and personal characteristics of supervisors
(average responses given below)

Personal Characteristics	Career Orientation		Total Average
	Supervisory	Managerial	
Age	31.60*	29.90	29.60
Father's occupational status†	4.45	4.57	4.48
Father's educational level‡	3.30*	3.59	3.43
Own occupational status†	3.54	3.60	3.56
Own educational level‡	3.78	3.84	3.87
Number of subordinates	3.80	2.90	3.50
Size of organization	272	286	282

* Significant above the 1 per cent level of confidence ($p < 0.01$)
† Occupational status:
1 = Higher professional and managerial
2 = Lower professional and managerial
3 = Supervisory and self-employed
4 = Clerical and sales
5 = Skilled trades
6 = Semi-skilled
7 = Unskilled
‡ Educational level:
1 = Some primary school
2 = Completed primary school
3 = Some secondary school
4 = Completed secondary school
5 = Some technical college
6 = Complete technical college

respondents with a "managerial" orientation tended to be younger, to possess higher educational qualifications, to have a clerical/sales background, and to work in larger organizations. Their fathers had worked mainly in managerial or professional occupations. Conversely, those respondents with a "supervisory" orientation tended to be older, to be less educationally qualified, to be drawn mainly from a skilled trade or unskilled background, and to work in smaller organizations. Their fathers, in the main, had worked in skilled trades or supervisory-level occupations. These differences were statistically significant only in terms of age and fathers' occupational background, but the trend of the results was apparent from the overall scores. It should also be noted that those respondents with a "managerial" orientation comprised approximately 20 per cent of the total sample.

The results of the study are supported by Dunkerley, who distinguished between "old style" and "new style" supervisors in Britain. The "old style" supervisor tended to be drawn from the ranks of blue-collar workers with a low level of formal education. The "new style" supervisor, by contrast, was a younger and more highly educated individual who often moved directly into supervision as the first step in a managerial career. In the United States it is not uncommon for young graduate engineers to be placed in supervisory or first-line management positions as part of their managerial training. Alternatively, supervision may be regarded as a "bridging occupation" which provides a stepping stone from a specialist occupation, such as engineering, to general management. "Old style" supervisors were reported by Dunkerley as regarding supervision as the peak of their career and to have a "local" or "organizational" orientation. "New style" supervisors, by contrast, tended to have a "cosmopolitan" or "external" orientation and to look for further advancement in a managerial career either within or outside their current organization.

These findings underline the importance of recognizing that supervisors are not homogeneous in their career orientations and that they are strongly influenced by their socio-economic background as well as their previous educational and occupational history. This has important implications for the training of supervisors and underlines the need to ensure that training programmes are designed to meet the needs, experience, and capabilities of particular groups of supervisors. It may not be appropriate, for example, to provide "old style" supervisors who do not aspire to a higher-level career in management with an advanced form of training. Conversely, "new style" supervisors with the capabilities and aspirations to move into the higher levels of organizations require more developmental forms of training.

3

Improving the Quality of First-Line Management

During the past few decades, numerous studies have been undertaken to measure and improve the quality of first-line management. In general, however, few of these studies have dealt effectively with the range and complexity of supervisory behaviour. Four main approaches to the study of supervisory effectiveness may be identified — as measured by the individual characteristics of supervisors, their work activities, their work situation, and the effects of supervision.

The individual characteristics of first-line managers. Psychologists have sought to measure the characteristics of supervisors in order to improve methods of selection, promotion, and the evaluation of training.[1] A typical example is a study by Roach,[2] which sought to classify the basic factors relevant to performance by an analysis of ratings by supervisors, peers, and subordinates. Another is a study by Dicken and Black,[3] which yielded seven "global" personal supervisory traits from a number of commonly used aptitude tests by asking psychologists to make clinical interpretations of the individual data. These were then correlated with field ratings and measured against actual success over a number of years. The results are shown in table 6. A major shortcoming of this approach is that it is unlikely that one type of personality or set of individual characteristics will be appropriate to every situation. Furthermore, the validity of much psychological research, especially where only a small number of cases are used, is open to question.

Table 6 Basic personal traits of supervisors

Personal Traits	Reported Reliability
Effective intelligence	0.98
Personal soundness	0.92
Drive and ambition	0.94
Leadership and dominance	0.90
Likeableness	0.86
Responsibility and conscientiousness	0.85
Ability to co-operate	0.86

Source: C.F. Dicken and J.D. Black, "Predictive Validity of Psychometric Evaluations of Supervisors", *Journal of Applied Psychology* 49 [1965]: 34-47.

Work activities of first-line managers. The second approach is to measure the work activities of supervisors. Four main methods are used to gather this type of data: (1) direct observation of supervisors on either a continuous basis, or by sampling their activities; (2) interviews with supervisors, which may be structured, semi-structured, or unstructured; (3) ratings made of a supervisor's activities by a researcher; and (4) questionnaires filled out by supervisors, including self-completed diaries. Any one of these methods may, of course, be used in combination with another.

The work situation of first-line managers. The third approach is to measure the supervisory work situation. This includes factors in the immediate environment which impinge on the supervisor's behaviour, as well as more general variables which have a long-term effect on the supervisor's role. Studies by Burns and Stalker,[4] Trist,[5] Woodward,[6] and others have demonstrated the importance of technological and environmental demands on organizational behaviour. This has been extended by Perrow,[7] who has suggested that some aspects of task structure are highly significant for supervisory behaviour. As shown in figure 5, Perrow distinguishes four types of organizational situation as measured by the degree of discretion (or choice of means) for supervisors compared with technical specialist staff, the degree of power (for example to mobilize resources) available to supervisors and technical staff, the type of co-ordination practised; and the degree of interdependence between groups. While

		Situations		
	A	B	C	D
Technical Control				
Discretion	Low	High	High	Low
Power	Low	High	High	High
Co-ordination	Planning	Feedback	Feedback	Planning
Interdependence of groups	Low	High	Low	Low
Supervision				
Discretion	High	High	Low	Low
Power	High	High	Low	Low
Co-ordination	Feedback	Feedback	Planning	Planning
Interdependence of groups	Low	High	Low	Low
EXAMPLES:	Shoe industry	Research and development (e.g., electronics)	Engineering industry	Steel industry

Source: C. Perrow, "A Framework for the Comparative Analysis of Organizations". *American Sociological Review* 32 [1967]: 194-208.

Figure 5   Types of organizational situation, corresponding to task structure

Perrow provides a useful kind of "map" which allows the work situation to be analyzed, it should be emphasized that task structure is only one aspect of the work situation.

The effects of supervisory behaviour. The fourth approach is to measure the effects of supervisory behaviour. Studies in the field have been among the least satisfactory in helping to improve the quality of supervision, mainly because of the fruitless search for general measures that can be applied to all supervisory situations. Thurley and Wirdenius,[8] however, have identified four typical situations, each of which require a different approach to measuring the effects of supervisory behaviour. These are set out in figure 6. In situation A, the stability of structural factors in the supervisory system facilitates the observation and testing of possible relationships between supervisory actions and a range of other criteria, such as production, labour turnover, costs, and so on. In situation B, it is not possible to isolate the effects of individual behaviour in any meaningful way. Thus the most appropriate method is to isolate certain actions of a group of supervisors as a whole and

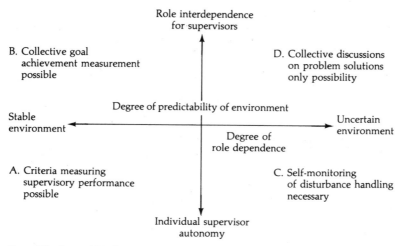

Source: Thurley and Wirdenius, *Supervision*, p. 109.

Figure 6 Evaluating the effects of supervision, according to different situations

test these against particular criteria of organizational effectiveness. In situation C, which deals with an autonomous supervisory role, it is useful to develop a systematic method of sampling cases of supervisory actions. In situation D, the emphasis is on the use of collective appraisal sessions, using external observers to collect data. According to studies conducted by Thurley and Wirdenius, the majority of supervisory situations fall into categories C and D.

The Training of First-Line Managers

Meade and Greig[9] believe that the development of supervisory training can be viewed as having passed through three historical stages. During the first stage, before the Second World War, there was an emphasis on the identification of intrinsic qualities within an individual that either made or marred him or her as a supervisor. Training was not an important issue, since the selection of supervisors was made on the basis of finding consistencies between a supervisor's personal qualities and the actual demands of the job. Thus, supervisors were regarded as "born and not made". The second stage was marked by the recognition that the work of supervisors involves the use of certain skills and knowledge which can be developed through training. This stage coincided with the emergence of the human relations movement, which stressed the importance of people as resources within organizations.[10] The third stage involved training through an analysis of the job itself and a preference for company-based training. Although supervisory training is still at this stage of development, according to Meade and Greig, there is considerable current debate about which components of the job should be analyzed, as well as how subsequent training should be conducted and by whom.

Identification of Training Needs among First-Line Managers

A number of steps need to be taken before any training programme is introduced. The first step involves determining the training needs of the supervisors in question as objectively as possible. This may involve analyzing what supervisors actually do in their jobs to ascertain the kind of skills and knowledge required. It may also be relevant to inquire into the various expectations individual supervisors have concerning their roles. Warr and Bird,[11] among others, stress that supervisors vary considerably in regard to their training needs.

The second step is to decide who should conduct the analysis of training needs. J.R. Armstrong[12] suggests that line managers should be involved from the outset, since they may have a particular view of what are the training needs of supervisors. Other commentators, however, feel that the analysis is best conducted by outside specialists who are emotionally detached from the day-to-day activities of supervisors. The supervisors themselves should also be involved as much as possible.

The third step is to choose the form the analysis should take. One method is to use job descriptions that give a broad outline of the supervisor's main tasks. Another is to undertake an activity analysis, such as diary keeping, observation, or activity sampling. The method used will depend on the resources available to the organization.

The fourth step is to undertake the actual assessment of training. This is, in fact, a continuous process which involves taking the objective results of job analysis, comparing these with the desired state of affairs, and then devising strategies for moving towards this desired state. Armstrong[13] suggests that the aspects most likely in need of development are technical competence, administrative skills, leadership abilities, and establishing relations between peer groups and superiors within an organization. The training needs that are identified will invariably take the form of objectives to be achieved. The setting of objectives may, in turn, be linked with a form of appraisal. Although traditional appraisal procedures tend to be conducted by supervisors of subordinates, there is a trend towards two-way appraisal which involves a more participative process.[14]

Establishing a Programme of Training and Education for
First-Line Managers

There are obviously many forms a training programme can take. One important choice is between internal, or enterprise-based, training and externally based training, which may be conducted at an outside institution. The advantages of the latter form of training are that it takes the supervisor away from the pressures of the work situation and may provide the opportunity for him or her to meet supervisors from other organizations. On the other hand, the internal training programme may be seen as having more relevance to the supervisor's immediate situation and is often less expensive in terms of time spent away from the job. Employers also tend to prefer enterprise-based training because it provides less opportunity for the supervisor to learn skills which are "transferable" and are therefore likely to encourage him or her to change jobs.

Thurley and Wirdenius put forward a seven-point plan for another approach to supervisory training.[15] In summary, their points are as follows. First, discussion of training needs to start from actual on-the-job problems. This will give the best clues about the priorities for a training programme. Second, an effective programme will involve all managers, staff, and supervisors who are in direct contact with the problems that have been identified. Third, all those involved in the programme should feel that they have been consulted in defining their training needs. Fourth, the methods used should involve a mixture of on-the-job discussions about problems between managers and supervisors, off-the-job discussions about work problems, and studies of job problems by third parties to discover objective information which can be fed back to the group for discussion. Fifth, training officers should act as catalysts to get the process under way, but the parties themselves should be responsible for the direction of the training programme. Sixth, supervisory training should be seen as a continuous activity for dealing with work problems and not as a "one-off" exercise. Seventh, all training needs cannot be met at once; they should proceed gradually, starting with the most urgent priorities and working through to those which are less pressing.

The Evaluation of First-Line Management Training

The assessment and evaluation of role performance in organizations become increasingly difficult as occupations become more complex. It is more difficult, for example, to assess the performance of a research scientist than to do so for an assembly-line worker. The same applies to the evaluation of training for more complex roles. The evaluation of supervisory training is therefore not a simple task. Meade and Greig[16] suggest that two factors need to be known in order to assess the effectiveness of supervisory training. First, there is information gained as a result of job analysis. Second, there is the extent to which the supervisors in question already possess the skills and knowledge defined as being necessary by the job analysis. One common form of evaluation is a "before-and-after" attitude test. In order to be rigorous, the attitudes of a control group would also need to be measured at two points in time, corresponding to "before" and "after", even though they were not exposed to the training programme. Similar tests could also be applied with regard to performance levels.

An important contribution to the evaluation of training has been made by Hesseling.[17] He argues that evaluation should be regarded as a strategy for both research and planned change. The object of evaluation should be to collect sufficient data to ensure that the direction of change can be controlled and any problems immediately recognized. Evaluation will involve different criteria and questions, according to who is evaluating and for whom the evaluation is taking place. Finally, all evaluation techniques have limitations and specific rather than general use. Hesseling warns against the adoption of prescriptive or "cook book" techniques of evaluation, since there is an enormous amount of variety in the nature of tasks and behaviour. On the other hand, there will be considerable benefits available using a strategy of evaluation designed to suit the situation in question.

The possibility of making some type of cost-benefit analysis of training is discussed by Thurley and Wirdenius.[18] A cost-benefit analysis is not a simple question of measurement and addition. The results will vary according to the person or group making the decision. A rational decision about whether to use a particular form of training can only be made if certain information is known about the situation in which it is to be applied. This includes the importance attached to training by the various parties involved, the perceived urgency of achieving benefits in the short or long run, the capacity of one party to impose its solution on others, and the relative amount of resources available in the immediate or long-term future. Given the unpredictability of the outcome of training, it is necessary to proceed with a strategy that periodically checks the costs and benefits, bearing in mind that there is no guarantee that predictions will be accurate. Thurley and Wirdenius note, however, that such an exercise at least provides "those who have to exercise judgement . . . a series of crude maps with possible routes across the difficult terrain".[19]

Extent of First-Line Management Training in Australia

Supervisory-level education and training has been a neglected field in Australia. In 1971, the Productivity Promotion Council of Australia conducted a survey of supervisory training among 930 organizations employing more than 400,000 people, including 50,000 supervisors. This represented approximately 10 per cent of the total Australian labour force. It was revealed that almost two-thirds of the supervisors in the survey had received no formal training in the previous twelve months. Of those who had been on supervisory training programmes, approximately half had received off-the-job training but within their organization, and one-third had received internal on-the-job training. Only 15 per cent had been sent by their organizations to an external course. It is interesting to note, however, that when asked which method of training they most favoured, approximately 37 per cent of employers nominated training at external institutions. Yet this was more than twice the proportion of supervisors who had actually received training of this kind.

A national survey of investment by private firms in training was conducted during 1976 under the joint sponsorship of the Australian Institute of Training and Development, the National Training Council, and the Department of Labour and Immigration. Information was obtained from 140 medium-size firms, drawn from a wide range of industries. The total expenditure on training by firms in the survey, on average, was $76,000, or $160 per employee. Expenditure varied considerably between occupational categories: from $360 per manager to $90 per supervisor. Indeed, supervisors received the lowest per capita expenditure on training among all occupations. In general, training received low priority, and only 23 per cent of employees in the firms surveyed received any training during the preceding year.

In our Technical and Further Education study, information about the training of supervisors was obtained from a national sample of 139 firms, mainly in the manufacturing sector. As shown in table 7, the most popular form of supervisory training

Table 7 Type of supervisory training and frequency of use (in percentages)

Type of Training	Frequency of Use		
	Regular	Irregular	Never
Internal or in-company	61	10	29
Management institute	20	31	49
Technical college	18	28	54
Employer organization	14	25	61
Government organization	9	28	63
Management consultant	2	20	78

Note: *Regular* includes "always" or "often".
  Irregular includes "seldom".
  Never includes "no planned training".

was conducted on an internal or in-company basis. Nevertheless, although 61 per cent of firms claimed to use this form of training on a regular basis, 29 per cent never provided internal training for supervisors. The second most popular form of training was through a management institute, such as the Australian Institute of Management. Institutes for Technical and Further Education (TAFE) were the third most popular provider, although 54 per cent of employers claimed that none of their supervision training was conducted through this means.

There were some curious anomalies in regard to employer attitudes towards TAFE courses in supervision. Approximately 90 per cent of firms claimed that they were aware of TAFE programmes and about half claimed that their supervisors were encouraged to enrol in these courses. Yet only 28 per cent of the supervisors in the survey claimed to have found out about TAFE courses from their employer and only 6 per cent indicated that they had been sent by their employer. Furthermore, although 46 per cent of the firms in the survey testified that supervision courses conducted by TAFE were "adequate" or "very adequate", only 18 per cent sent their supervisors to these courses on a regular basis. Thus it would appear that while most employers paid lip-service to the value of TAFE courses, only a small minority were prepared to encourage their supervisors to attend courses that were offered.

The TAFE institutes are the only sector of post-secondary education in Australia in which courses in supervision are offered. There is some variation between states, but most offer a two-year certificate-level qualification. The first year of the course usually comprises a general introduction to supervision with an emphasis on "human relations" and "supervision techniques". The number of lecturer contact hours varies from two hours a week (in Western Australia) to four hours a week (in Victoria, South Australia, and Tasmania). The second year tends to allow specialization within a particular field of supervision, such as industrial, office, or retail. In general, however, the content of these courses tends to have remained fairly static over the years and to reflect the concerns of supervision in the 1950s and 1960s rather than the present day.

Survey respondents who were then enrolled in a TAFE supervision course tended to be fairly uncritical of the programme offered. Approximately half felt that it was relevant to their everyday work and that the TAFE institutes adequately met the needs of supervisory education. Almost two-thirds felt that the course was important for their future career, and more than three-quarters agreed that their teachers had a good understanding of the supervisor's job. By contrast, however, less than one-third felt that employers regarded the TAFE supervision course as an essential part of their training and development. Thus, there appeared to be a discrepancy between the intrinsic value which students claimed to derive from the course and the lack of credibility TAFE had with employers.

A follow-up study of 147 supervisors approximately one year after they completed their supervision certificate provided some insights into problems of the TAFE courses. According to these respondents, only about one-third of those who enrolled in the certificate course actually completed their studies. The main factors they ascribed to this high drop-out rate were boredom with the course and job pressures. There were several major reasons given by those who completed the course, however, which helped to explain their persistence. These tended to emphasize the belief that completion of the programme enhanced their promotion prospects or improved their job mobility. Most had not been given the opportunity within

their employing organizations to undertake supervision training, and a majority claimed that they planned to undertake
further management training as the result of completing the
certificate.

It would appear, therefore, that only a minority of those
entering a supervision course at a TAFE institute ever obtain a
certificate. Those who do so tend to have strong individual
motivation and to be oriented to a higher managerial career.
They also tend to be individuals who feel that their potential
has not been recognized by their employer and seek to obtain
the TAFE certificate in order to prove their ability. This is
despite their lack of expectation that the qualification will be
given any recognition by their employer.

*Training Future First-Line Managers: Implications for
Educational Institutions*

It is apparent from the findings of the study that the training of
supervisors in Australia has proceeded in a piecemeal and
haphazard fashion. A major issue is the future role of TAFE
institutes in this field. Clearly, TAFE only provides direct training for a small minority of first-line managers in Australia, yet it
is the only post-secondary level institution that offers courses in
this area. While employers pay lip-service to the importance of
supervisory training, they have generally neglected the needs
of this group. The lack of attention given to the needs of first-
line managers by both employers and governments is in
marked contrast to their high degree of involvement in other
areas of training and education. There is general consensus that
governments and employers should co-operate in the training
of skilled workers in order to maintain and improve the standards of Australian industry. In recent years both universities
and colleges of advanced education have become increasingly
involved in providing management education. Yet similar
recognition has not been given to the importance of training the
first-line manager at either enterprise or industry level.

The appropriate design of education and training programmes for supervisors is intertwined with the likely future role of

the supervisor. As already noted, there is considerable debate about the long-term consequences of current social, economic, and technological changes for the supervisor. Thurley and Wirdenius, for example, set out several possible directions for the future. Firstly, supervision may "wither away" and be replaced by a more "democratic" system in which workers will be self-managing or autonomous. Secondly, supervision may become increasingly "professionalized" and be given greater authority in increasingly bureaucratic forms of organization. Thirdly, supervision may be transformed into a system of temporary problem-solving teams which preserve the "production" functions but remove the current status differentiations between supervisors and operatives.

If TAFE is to play an expanded role in meeting the needs of future first-line managers, the courses offered will have to be sufficiently flexible to adapt to possible changes in the role of the supervisor. TAFE will also have to improve its credibility among both employers and potential students. The direction in which the TAFE institutes move will be the result of various pressures from government, employers, educationalists, and, it is to be hoped, from supervisors themselves. In order to anticipate possible developments, three alternatives are briefly considered and some assessment made of their likely consequences for first-line management.

The first alternative is for the TAFE institutes to continue with their current Certificate of Supervision with few or no changes. From the foregoing analysis it is unlikely that this course of action would be satisfactory to anyone. Employers are likely to remain indifferent to TAFE courses, and students will continue to express their lack of motivation by either failing to enrol or dropping out before completing the course.

A second alternative is to upgrade the existing courses to middle-management level. This would also mean raising the entrance qualifications and moving to courses of longer duration. Such a development has the support of many teachers and administrators in the TAFE sector, who see this as a means of enhancing the status of TAFE institutes. It would, however, merely duplicate courses that are currently conducted within the colleges of advanced education and universities. It would also abandon the field of supervision training to employers and private agencies. Furthermore, it would neglect the needs of students who use the TAFE courses as a way of obtaining a "second chance" of entering higher education.

A third alternative is to completely restructure the current TAFE courses in supervision to provide attractive and educationally meaningful programmes. It should be possible for TAFE to develop a set of courses at the supervision level which would enable students to achieve their objectives more satisfactorily than at present. TAFE could also develop multifaceted programmes which would facilitate a better integration of the needs of individual supervisors with those of their employers. A lead in this direction has been provided by the Research and Planning Branch of TAFE in South Australia, which has designed a variety of training modules for use in both institutes and industry. Some TAFE institutes have also begun to collaborate with employers on a combination of in-plant training and classroom activities; although administrative structures within TAFE tend to inhibit this process. Another aspect that demands attention is the relationship between the different sectors of post-secondary education in the management field. Courses should be more closely integrated so that students can pass more easily from TAFE to other sectors or, indeed, choose subjects offered by different institutions where this fits their needs.[20]

PART 2

MODELS FOR CHANGE

4

The Human Resources Approach

The writings of both Douglas McGregor[1] and Rensis Likert[2] have strongly influenced programmes of organizational change which emphasize the importance of leadership style and work-group behaviour. Both writers were American social psychologists who published significant books in the 1960s which strongly influenced a generation of managerial thinking. The dominant theme in writings of both was that effective organizations comprise interacting groups of people with "supportive relationships" to each other. The task of management is to ensure that employees feel that their organization's objectives are of significance to them, that their jobs are meaningful, and that they have support from their superiors. McGregor undertook most of his research while at the Sloan School of Management at the Massachusetts Institute of Technology, while Likert was associated mainly with the Institute for Social Research at the University of Michigan.

McGregor was concerned with the assumptions about human behaviour that underlie managerial actions. He argued that the traditional conceptions of management were based upon the direction and control by management of the enterprise and of its individual members. McGregor dubbed this approach as Theory X. By contrast, Theory Y sought to replace direction and control by management with the principal of "integration", whereby employees became willing partners with management and exercised self-direction in the service of objectives to which they were committed. McGregor urged that

Figure 7 Profile of organizational characteristics

	ORGANIZATIONAL VARIABLES	SYSTEM 1	SYSTEM 2	SYSTEM 3 Substantial amount	SYSTEM 4	Item no.
LEADERSHIP	How much confidence and trust is shown in subordinates?	Virtually none	Some	Substantial amount	A great deal	1
	How free do they feel to talk to superiors about job?	Not very free	Somewhat free	Quite free	Very free	2
	How often are subordinates' ideas sought and used constructively?	Seldom	Sometimes	Often	Very frequently	3
MOTIVATION	Is predominant use made of 1 fear, 2 threats, 3 punishment, 4 rewards, 5 involvement?	1, 2, 3, occasionally 4	4, some 3	4, some 3 and 5	5, 4, based on group	4
	Where is responsibility felt for achieving organization's goals?	Mostly at top	Top and middle	Fairly general	At all levels	5
	How much cooperative teamwork exists?	Very little	Relatively little	Moderate amount	Great deal	6
COMMUNICATION	What is the usual direction of information flow?	Downward	Mostly downward	Down and up	Down, up, and sideways	7
	How is downward communication accepted?	With suspicion	Possibly with suspicion	With caution	With a receptive mind	8
	How accurate is upward communications?	Usually inaccurate	Often inaccurate	Often accurate	Almost always accurate	9
	How well do superiors know	Not very well	Rather well	Quite well	Very well	

DECISIONS

At what level are decisions made?				
Are subordinates involved in decisions related to their work?	Almost never	Occasionally consulted	Generally consulted	Fully involved
What does decision-making process contribution to motivation?	Not very much	Relatively little	Some contribution	Substantial contribution

GOALS

How are organizational goals established?	Orders issued	Orders, some comments invited	After discussion, by orders	By group action (except in crisis)
How much covert resistance to goals is present?	Strong resistance	Moderate resistance	Some resistance at times	Little or none

CONTROL

How concentrated are review and control functions?	Very highly at top	Quite highly at top	Moderate delegation to lower levels	Widely shared
Is there an informal organization resisting the formal one?	Yes	Usually	Sometimes	No - - - same goals as formal
What are cost, productivity, and other control data used for?	Policing, punishment	Reward and punishment	Reward, some self-guidance	Self-guidance, problem-solving

11 12 13 14 15 16 17 18

(Adapted from R. Likert, *The Human Organization: Its Management and Value.* [New York: McGraw-Hill, 1967], pp. 197-211.)

supervisors should exercise a general rather than detailed control over the job and be more concerned with targets than methods. They should adopt high performance goals, facilitate a higher degree of employee participation in decision-making, and be "employee centred" rather than "job centred" in their approach.

Rensis Likert also investigated the effect of various management styles on organizational performance and found that the best results occurred where supervisors focused their attention on the human aspects of their subordinates' problems and on building effective work groups which were set high achievement goals. Supervisors who were "employee centred" attempted to get to know their subordinates as individuals and saw their primary function as assisting others to perform their work more efficiently. Likert developed a "self reporting" questionnaire which enabled employees to rate their organization in terms of various operating characteristics such as leadership style, motivation, communication, decision-making, and control processes. Sample items from Likert's questionnaire are shown in figure 7.

In summarizing the findings of his research, Likert distinguished four systems of management. System 1 is an "exploitive-authoritative" type in which management relies on fear and threats, communication is downward, there is a strong distinction made between supervisors and subordinates, and decision-making is highly centralized. System 2 is a "benevolent-authoritarian" type, in which management uses rewards but subordinates remain subservient, communications are restricted by management, and there is only limited delegation of authority. System 3 is a "consultative type" in which communications are two-way but limited, subordinates have a moderate influence on decision-making, but policy-making is confined to those at the top of the organization. System 4 is characterized as "participative group management", since full use is made of group participation and involvement in decision-making. Management also provides substantial rewards for employees in accordance with their level of performance, there is open and free communication between all levels within the organization, and there is a strong emphasis on group relationships.

In studies of numerous organizations, Likert reported that the closer the management style was to system 4, the more likely it was to have a continuous record of high productivity. In one study conducted by Likert in the clothing industry, an unprofitable enterprise was taken over by a more successful company. At the time of the take-over, the unprofitable firm was using a management style that fell approximately between systems 1 and 2. Changes implemented by the new owners included different methods of work, improved maintenance of machinery, and a training programme for employees at all levels of the organization. Supervisors were also encouraged to adopt the system 4 style of management. Within two years, the level of productivity rose by almost 30 per cent, costs declined by 20 per cent, and morale rose considerably. The company's public image improved, and it showed a profit for the first time in many years.

An important aspect of system 4 is the development of overlapping work groups, which are linked together both vertically and laterally by individuals who perform a "linking pin" function, as illustrated in figure 8. The dots in the overlapping

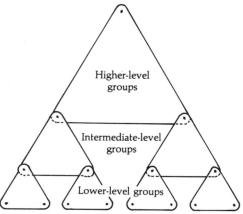

(Reproduced, by permission, from R. Likert, *New Patterns of Management* [New York: McGraw-Hill, 1961], p. 110.)

Figure 8   Interlocking work groups

corners of the figure represent the linking pins in the organization. Those providing "vertical linkage" tend to occupy a supervisory position in their work group and are also members of a group at the next highest level in the organizational hierarchy. In this position, they are able to pass decisions and information from one level to the next. Those who provide the "lateral or horizontal linkage" are members of more than one group. Their role is to ensure, where possible, that each group is aware of actions and decisions taken in other areas. In figure 8 there are two members of each group with overlapping membership of another. However, any number of combinations is possible, depending on the size of the group.

An example of interlocking work groups is provided by a Brisbane hospital with over a thousand staff members.[3] For some years the hospital's chief administrator had been concerned about lack of staff interest in the hospital's objectives and blurred lines of communication, delegation, and decision-making. The staff also complained about impersonal management. The administrator felt that many of these problems could be overcome by changing the organization structure to enable staff to participate in decisions that affected their work areas. A consultant was engaged by the hospital to assist in the reorganization. After interviewing a wide cross-section of the staff, the consultant recommended the formation of linked work groups throughout the hospital. A training programme was conducted for middle management to acquaint them with the problems and to seek possible methods of resolution. As a result, a new organizational structure, based upon the linked work group concept, was evolved.

The shape of the new hospital structure is shown in figure 9. The top and second tier groups are linked together along the lines suggested by Likert. Following the Likert model, the organization is linked vertically by the co-ordinators of each service group, who are members of the executive management board. They provide a means of passing information from the top to middle levels of the organization. The three service groups, in turn, are linked laterally by representatives, who attend each other's meetings. In this way, for example, one

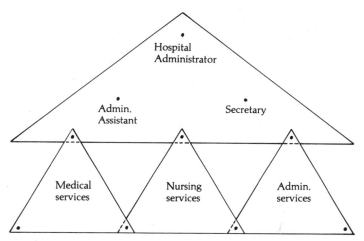

(Reproduced, by permission, from R. Smith, "Linked Work Groups Bridge the Communications Gap", *Work and People* 1, no. 2 [1975], p. 4.)

Figure 9   Vertical and lateral interlocking groups in a Brisbane hospital.

member of the nursing service group is also part of the medical service group, while another holds joint membership of the administrative service groups.

The executive management board is in charge of the day-to-day management of the hospital and meets two or three times a week. It conducts formal meetings to which members submit items for discussion. If full consensus is not obtained, decisions are reached by a majority vote. The frequency of meetings held by the three service groups is determined by the members, but most meet weekly or fortnightly. Minutes of all group meetings are forwarded to the executive management board. Evaluation of the operation of the new structure has so far been informal, although it is intended to conduct periodic assessments in the future.

Another application of the linked work groups occurred in the large retail firm of David Jones Limited.[4] The company found that there was poor co-ordination between specific areas. The sales side of the organization, for example, was poorly informed about what the buying side was doing and as a consequence had very little product knowledge. Similar problems were evident between other sections of the company, which led to inadequate decision-making by middle-management personnel.

The decision to restructure the organization on a linked work group basis resulted from a meeting of senior management with a consultant on organizational design. As shown in figure 10, the top executive group now includes the managers of five different functional areas. Meetings of the executive are held weekly and follow an agenda, to which all group members may contribute items. Minutes of the meeting are recorded and circulated to all members of the group. Second- and third-level groups were subsequently formed along the same lines as the executive group. After twelve months of experience with the linked work groups, the company conducted a further revision of its organizational structure. This involved removing one tier of management at the senior-controller level in order to improve co-ordination between the purchasing and sales divisions of the company.

(Reproduced, by permission, from R. Smith, "Linked Work Groups Bridge the Communications Gap", p. 5.)

Figure 10   Vertical interlocking groups in a retail organization

One of the main reasons for introducing linked work groups at David Jones was to improve communications between functional areas. The new organization structure is based on consideration of who should *communicate* with whom, rather than who should *report* to whom. More effective lateral communication links have been developed by encouraging people to make direct contact with others at their own level, in other parts of the organization, who can give them the information they require. This has been facilitated by laterally linked groups, which use the same group meeting procedures as vertical groups but can transmit information across the organization more effectively. Using the two-way linked groups, for example, the personnel manager not only has contact vertically, with the top executive group, but also has lateral contact with managers of other sections in the organization.

A survey of staff opinion was conducted in both the hospital and the retail organizations to ascertain the general attitudes to the linked group scheme. Approximately 90 per cent of the respondents stated that the linked groups had assisted them in the jobs. Nevertheless, there were some problems. These included the time taken up by group meetings, inadequate follow-up and feedback procedures, decisions still being made at too high a level in the organization, and problems arising in group discussion which were unrelated to work. The linked group concept, however, was found to have strong advantages in the following areas. Firstly, it led to improved communication by giving members more opportunity to discuss problems with one another. Secondly, it provided employees with better knowledge of the organization and understanding of the problems of other sections and departments. FInally, it made decision-making easier because more information was made available. In summary, the formation of overlapping work groups was initially time consuming and slow to yield substantial results; once established, however, the groups provided greater job satisfaction and yielded improved organizational performance. The long-term effectiveness of linked groups, nevertheless, depends on periodic evaluation and adjustment of faults to ensure their smooth operation.

Both McGregor and Likert have been criticised for being highly prescriptive and over-selective in their use of evidence.[5] The theoretical foundations of their theories, it is argued, are grounded in the "neo-human relations approach" which conceptualizes organizations as co-operative systems in which it is the task of management to integrate the goals of individual workers with those of the organization. Conflict within organizations is seen as emanating from interpersonal differences rather than from social or economic conditions. Critics have also highlighted the predominantly "managerial" orientation of both McGregor and Likert, which assumes that harmony will be achieved simply by encouraging interaction between superiors and subordinates. Criticism is also levelled at the broad generalizations that have been drawn from studies of small-group or individual interactions and applied to large-scale organizations. Finally, it is difficult to validate claims that organizational change or increased levels of employee satisfaction and productivity have been due solely to the adoption of managerial styles or structures advocated by McGregor and Likert.

Notwithstanding the criticisms made of the theories espoused by McGregor and Likert, the "human resources" approach has been an important basis for experiments in organizational change which has resulted in a re-evaluation of the role of the first-line manager. The following two case studies are based upon programmes of change conducted by General Motors in the United States and Australia. Although the activities reported in these case studies were conducted under the heading of General Motors' Quality of Work Life programme, they have their origin in the "human resources" approach of Likert and McGregor. The studies provide useful illustrations of the strengths and limitations of an influential approach to organizational change which has been applied in a wide variety of settings. Particular attention should be paid to the implications of these theories for the role of the first-line manager.

Case 1: The Lakewood Plant

In the 1970s, General Motors opened a new assembly plant in the United States at Lordstown, Ohio. It was described as the world's fastest and most technologically sophisticated automobile assembly line. Almost from its inception, however, the Lordstown plant was the object of strikes and sabotage, which led to it becoming a *cause célèbre*. The "Lordstown Syndrome" became a symbol of worker discontent on automated assembly lines in the United States. General Motors' management denied the widespread impression that the Lordstown dispute represented a revolt by younger, more educated workers against the monotony and pressures of the assembly line. Rather, they argued, the strike was over work standards created by the consolidation of two corporate divisions and the subsequent merger of two union branches. The United Auto Workers Union (UAW), however, contended that the main issue in dispute concerned increases in the speed of the assembly line and the laying-off of workers. According to a thirty-year-old UAW representative, who led the strike at Lordstown, the dispute occurred because workers felt that their jobs were inhumanely dull and the pressures too great. In his words: "The attitude of young people is going to compel management to make jobs more desirable in the workplace and to fulfil the needs of people."

The Quality of Work Life Programme at General Motors

In the aftermath of the Lordstown dispute, General Motors instituted a wide-ranging programme to improve the quality of work life (QWL) for employees in its plants. The QWL concept is very broad but was defined by General Motors as including the following issues:
1. A satisfying and productive work environment
2. Improved communications between supervision and employees
3. Development of teamwork
4. Improved employee self-confidence and leadership
5. Better understanding of job requirements by employees
6. Opportunities for employees to use creativity and problem-solving skills relevant to their work

Although the QWL improvement programme initiated by General Motors did not seek to radically restructure the total organization or relationships between employees and management, it indicated a concern by the company to avoid the Lordstown syndrome at other plants. The UAW co-operated with General Motors in a number of QWL ventures. The general strategy adopted by General Motors was to encourage individual plants to adopt their own approach rather than follow a particular blueprint for change.

The Lakewood Plant

One of the first projects aimed at QWL improvement was undertaken at the Lakewood assembly plant in Atlanta, Georgia. Using the results of an organizational survey technique, developed by Rensis Likert, the plant was identified as operating under "benevolent authoritarian" principles. A new plant manager was transferred to Lakewood who set about changing the organization to one that operated according to "participative group" management principles. The main emphasis of the Lakewood programme was on providing greater information to all employees and encouraging them to participate in decisions that concerned their job. Employees received information on a wide range of subjects such as future products, organizational changes, selected cost data, quality, and efficiency, most of which had previously been regarded as confidential. In addition, employees were provided with feedback on a regular basis concerning their performance compared with similar General Motors plants elsewhere.

Changing the Supervisor's Role at Lakewood

Another major change was the redefinition of the supervisor's job by adopting a "planned leadership" concept. Essentially, this consisted of providing production supervisors with "utility trainers" to assist them with non-supervisory functions, such as training new and reassigned employees, trouble-shooting quality problems, rearranging operations, controlling salvage, picking up tools and supplies from stores, checking fixtures, and so on. This enabled the supervisors to concentrate on their primary role of being effective managers of people. "Follow-up people" were also assigned on a full-time basis to ensure that the utility trainers functioned properly and implemented their new roles. It took approximately a year for the full benefits of the changes to be felt in the Lakewood organization. Supervisors encountered problems in practising their roles as well as meeting resistance from within the existing organizational system. As one supervisor commented: "I've got more time to be a better manager, but I can't get the organization to respond."

Team Development

Another aspect of the Lakewood project involved the development of "cross-functional business teams". This occurred within the "cushion room", a department with 250 employees, where production and service functions were brought together and encouraged to function as a separate business enterprise. All employees were invited to participate in setting goals and developing strategies for achieving them. The general supervisor in the cushion room functioned as the leader of a team that included a quality-control specialist and staff people from production engineering, plant engineering, industrial relations, materials handling, and accounting. The group met every day, either at lunchtime or after work (for which the members received overtime payments). The teams set goals in the areas of production, scrap, grievances, and so on that were more demanding than any higher management would have presumed to set for them, and then went on to meet or exceed their set of self-determined goals. Continuous feedback was considered essential to the success of the team development programme. Special charts, which were often changed on a daily basis, showed all the employees how the cushion room ranked against similar operations in other plants in terms of absenteeism, efficiency, quality, scrap costs, and housekeeping items.

Results of the Lakewood Project

At the end of the first year, a survey of attitudes among employees at Lakewood showed an increase in a wide range of "human organization" scores. These included variables such as organizational climate, supervisory leadership, and job satisfaction. However, while the human organization improved, productivity and costs deteriorated. A number of reasons were advanced to explain this phenomenon. First, improvements in human organization required initial outlays on increased manpower, training, and facility changes. Second, and more important, it takes time for improved management practices to be accepted and implemented, time for improved management practices to be reflected in improved employee attitudes, and still more time for these improved attitudes to be reflected in improved performance.

After the second year of the project, as shown in figure 11, direct labour efficiency showed a sizable improvement, and the trend continued thereafter. Improvement in indirect labour efficiencies had to wait until the third year, but the overall improvement in plant efficiency over the three-year period from

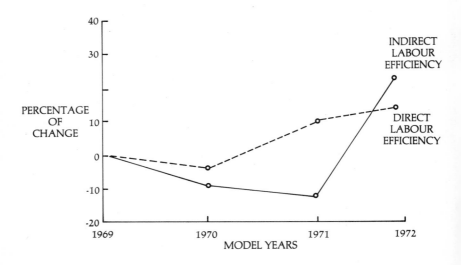

the inception of the project was considerable. Furthermore, there were other savings such as reduced tool breakage, lower scrap costs, and improved quality. In the cushion room, where attention was given to team development, a substantial reduction in labour costs was achieved. Scrap declined to less than one-quarter of the previous level, and there was a 50 per cent decrease in the number of written grievances presented by employees against the company.

The Lessons of the Lakewood Project

One question that arose from the Lakewood experience was: To what degree were the results achieved at Lakewood typical? For example, it took almost five years to achieve similar improvements in productivity, costs, and profits in another plant where the initial situation was not unlike that at Lakewood. It should also be noted that the initial objective of achieving full participative group management at Lakewood was only partly realized. The attainment of this goal would have required each work group to make all the major decisions that affected it, all members of the work group to participate in making these decisions, and, finally, all decisions to be made by consensus. Nevertheless, a number of improvements were made in this direction, and the Lakewood project does provide an indication of results that can be achieved from concerted effort by management to improve the quality of work life.

The following general conclusions concerning the ingredients required for successful organizational change may be drawn from the Lakewood project:

1. *Active participation is required by top management in any changes.* Mere commitment and support are not enough. This was certainly the case at Lakewood, where the plant manager was closely involved in the change programme.
2. *There is no all-purpose set of tools to improve the effectiveness of any organization.* At Lakewood, the principal tools were information and feedback on both human organization and productive efficiency, team building, the planned leadership con-

cept, and participation in the preparation for model changes.

3. *Change in attitudes to interpersonal relations should be accompanied by appropriate changes in structure.* At Lakewood, interpersonal strategies such as team building and goal setting were combined with structural changes such as the provision of "utility trainers" to assist supervisors and the establishment of cross-functional business teams.

4. *Top management must grant greater autonomy to employees in decision-making.* This was the case in the cushion room, where the teams were semi-autonomous in terms of work flow. Limitations of technology, however, prevented the concept being applied to other areas of the plant.

5. *Employees who are affected by anticipated changes should be involved in decisions governing these changes.* At Lakewood, this principal was observed in the cushion room project, where employees were involved from the beginning. Broad outlines of suggested changes were made by management, but the advice of employees was sought in implementing the contemplated changes and opportunities were given for introducing modifications.

6. *People require frequent feedback to prove that they have changed in ways that benefit both themselves and the organization.* Studies of adult learning processes indicate that people need to experiment with new approaches and receive appropriate feedback or reinforcement in the on-the-job situation. This principle was followed most closely in the cushion room, where feedback was given almost on a daily basis. The teams in the cushion room did not suffer the lag between improved human organization and improved efficiency which characterized other parts of the plant, where feedback was less frequent.

Certainly the changes experienced at Lakewood were less dramatic than those achieved at the Kalmar plant of Volvo (see chap. 7). No attempt was made to alter the automated high-speed production line at Lakewood towards the concept of group assembly as practised by Volvo at Kalmar. Indeed, according to the plant manager at Lakewood, who visited Kalmar and other similar plants in Sweden, the concept of group assembly is more appropriate to low-volume production situations. Nevertheless, the Lakewood project demonstrates that considerable achievements in improving the quality of work life are possible even within the constraints of assembly-line technology.

Case 2: The Elizabeth Plant

A programme of organizational change was instituted by General Motors–Holden's (GMH) at the Elizabeth assembly plant in the mid-1970s. This study describes the approach taken by GMH, which may usefully be compared with both the Lakewood and Kalmar cases. At Elizabeth, the major emphasis was upon upgrading the effectiveness of first-line management rather than embarking upon a radical change in the design of work and organization as occured at Kalmar. Nevertheless, the consequences of change were highly significant for the role of the supervisor in the enterprise. Unlike Volvo, GMH was not seeking to eliminate or change traditional supervisory roles, although changes were introduced which might eventually lead to a new style of management at the shop-floor level.

The Elizabeth assembly plant was almost twenty years old and had a labour force of approximately sixteen hundred. During the early 1970s, performance declined to such an extent that GMH proposed closing the plant and moving production elsewhere. An investigation undertaken by GMH, in collaboration with a firm of consultants, revealed no single cause underlying the problems at the plant but rather a complex array of factors. As shown in figure 12, a vicious circle of production pressures on supervisors and managers led to solutions based on expediency which in turn led to a general atmosphere of insecurity and low morale.

Industrial relations deteriorated to an all-time low of more than twenty individual work stoppages in one year. Many of the strikes were unofficial, or wildcat, in that they were undertaken by shop-floor workers without the official support of the

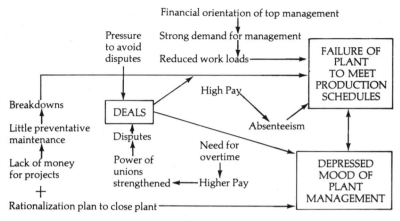

(Adapted from R.E. Ault, "A Model for Initiating Change in Large Social Systems", Ed.D. thesis, Western Michigan University, 1977.)

Figure 12   An analysis of problems at the Elizabeth plant

respective union officials. The situation was complicated by the structure of unionism in the Australian vehicle-building industry. At the Elizabeth assembly plant there were seventeen separate unions covering all employees up to and including superintendent level. During the 1970s, employers in the Australian vehicle industry unsuccessfully contested a long legal case in which the Association of Drafting, Supervisory and Technical Employees (ADSTE) sought coverage, under the Australian Conciliation and Arbitration Act, of all supervisory-level employees in the industry. The High Court eventually ruled that the ADSTE had the right to organize supervisors in the vehicle-building industry. Although this was not a major cause of industrial unrest at Elizabeth, it was an important background variable in the situation and led to the unionization of supervisors at the plant.

The Strategy for Organizational Change at Elizabeth

As a result of a three-day off-site conference among senior management from the Elizabeth plant, a list of organizational goals was drawn up which became the basis for a subsequent action programme. The agreed goals were to create an organization in which —

(a) authority and responsibility for running the plant should be shared by the salaried employees;

(b) mutual trust should be developed between salaried and hourly employees;

(c) commonly agreed goals would be established for the plant;

(d) people would be involved in the making of decisions that affected them;

(e) there would be freedom for creativity;

(f) employees would be able to maintain their dignity at work;

(g) everyone would be prepared to help each other.

The strategy for seeking to implement these goals was divided into two phases. In phase 1, action was focused on raising the morale and effectiveness of the management and supervisory group. This was seen as a prerequisite for phase 2, in which the quality of work life experienced by hourly paid employees would be improved and better relationships between management and employees would be fostered.

A number of structural and production changes were also undertaken at the Elizabeth plant in order to improve performance. Assembly management, for example, were given more direct responsibility for maintenance and quality control. Preventive maintenance projects and action on manufacturing change requests were given higher priority than had previously been the case. Increased investment was made in the assembly plant. Supervisors were also involved in discussions, similar to those which had been initiated among top management, to enable them to contribute ideas to the overall strategy for change. The supervisors identified further actions which could be undertaken at the shop-floor level in order to improve morale and raise productivity. These included projects on vehicle damage control, paint processing and scheduling.

The "top-down" strategy employed by GMH was in contrast to the approach used by Volvo at Kalmar. This difference may be partly explained in terms of the industrial relations system within Australian industry. The dominance of the arbitration system has meant that negotiations between unions and employees tend to be conducted within the tribunals rather than at a plant level. The concept of "managerial prerogatives" is strongly entrenched within the Australian system, and employers are generally reluctant to share decision-making with employees. For their part, Australian unions are accustomed to confining their actions to questions of improving the pay and conditions of their members rather than becoming involved in issues such as work restructuring or joint decision-making.

Changing the Role of the Supervisor at Elizabeth

As part of the organizational change strategy at Elizabeth, supervisors were given greater responsibility for management at the departmental level. In one section of the plant, in the trim and body shops, the three supervisory levels began to meet and make group decisions on departmental goals, operations, and long-term planning. This meant that the supervisors became more involved in matters beyond their immediate area and were able to see how their activities were linked with others. It also enabled supervisors to become more directly involved in influencing decisions that affected their areas of activity, such as developing plans for the introduction of a second shift in the plant.

GMH upgraded the training programme given to supervisors at the plant. A twelve-month full-time pre-supervisory training course was introduced for hourly paid employees who were identified as having management potential. Leading hands were given training not only in supervision but in broader aspects of plant operations. Supervisors participated in the design of their own training programme. An inventory of current skills, knowledge, and experience required by supervisors was drawn up and compared with expected future demands. As a result of this exercise, a new supervisory training programme was designed which included group skills, problem and decision analysis, counselling, industrial relations, and various other subjects. The programme entailed a total of 120 hours training per supervisor. The objective of the programme was to upgrade the skills of supervisors as well as involve them in long-term organizational planning.

Evaluating the Changes at Elizabeth

The main focus of activity at Elizabeth was upon improving the effectiveness of first-line management and represented phase 1 of a long-term strategy for change. A survey undertaken by GMH indicated that the plant achieved the second-highest overall quality of work life score among seven manufacturing units. This was a significant improvement from the previous period when the plant had been threatened with closure. Performance at the plant improved greatly in the three years following the introduction of the programme. Budget efficiency rose by 13 per cent, the average quality index score increased by 9 per cent, and the average daily under achievement of schedule declined to one per day.

Major issues that remained unresolved, however, included various structural and technological changes which would be necessary to ensure the survival of the plant in the future. This would require close collaboration between the management and the unions to minimize social and economic dislocation. It could require a more radical series of industrial and organizational changes than had hitherto been attempted. The future would also be governed by many decisions which were beyond the control of the plant manager and were central to the continued existence of the Australian vehicle-assembly industry.

5

The Grid Organization Development Approach

The concept of organizational development through the "Managerial Grid" originated with two American psychologists, Robert Blake and Jane Mouton, in the 1960s and has subsequently been used in many other countries.[1] Blake and Mouton argued that the manager should foster attitudes and behaviour that promote efficient performance, generate enthusiasm for experimentation and innovation, and result in learning from interaction with others. The Managerial Grid, designed by Blake and Mouton, provides a framework for understanding and learning a pattern of managerial behaviour which the authors regard as essential for achieving an effective organization. The Managerial Grid results from combining two fundamental ingredients of managerial behaviour: concern for production and concern for people. *Concern for* does not indicate dedication to specific targets or the results achieved in themselves. Rather, it means a general approach to management which should govern the actions of supervisors or managers in terms of *how* they concern themselves with production and with people.

Concern for production refers not only to physical factory products but also to the number of good research ideas, the number of accounts processed, volume of sales, quality of service given, and so on. Similarly, concern for people includes regard for friendships, personal commitment to tasks, self-respect, equitable payment, and the like. How managers approach their role, according to Blake and Mouton, will show more or less of these two fundamental constituents. Placing these two fundamentals as axes on a graph, as shown in figure 13, enables a grid to be drawn which reveals many typical combinations of managerial behaviour.

The grid indicates that all degrees of concern for production and people are possible; but, for simplicity, five styles of management are highlighted for comparison. Firstly, "task management" (9, 1) focuses overwhelmingly on production, subordinates are expected to do what they are told, and any disagreements are suppressed. Secondly, "country-club management" (1, 9) is solely concerned about people; management tries to avoid disagreement with or criticism of staff, and production problems are glossed over. Thirdly, "impoverished management" (1, 1) is characterized by the avoidance of personal responsibility or personal commitment; management

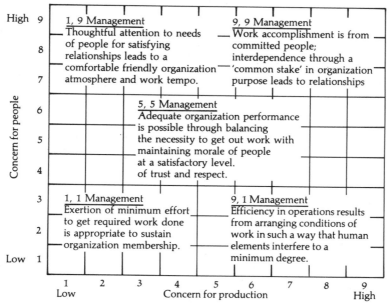

(Reproduced, by permission, from R. Blake and J. Mouton, *The Managerial Grid* [Houston: Gulf Publishing Co., 1964], p. 10.)

Figure 13   The Managerial Grid

allows employees to work as they see fit, without any assistance or guidance. Fourthly, "middle-of-the-road management" (5, 5) exerts sufficient pressure to gain acceptable production levels but yields enough to maintain adequate morale; management splits the difference where problems arise with employees and seeks balanced solutions rather than the most appropriate ones. Finally, "team management" (9, 9) aims at the highest attainable production in which everyone finds his own sense of accomplishment; problems are confronted directly and openly, and conflict is accepted; objectives set by management are clear and realistic; employees satisfy their own needs through the job and working with others.

Blake and Mouton advocate a systematically phased programme of organization development which will move the style of management towards a 9, 9 position of concern for both people and production. The programme consists of six phases. In phase 1, participants are introduced to the Managerial Grid through laboratory-seminar training. In phase 2, teams of small groups are formed using a "diagonal slice" of the organization's membership. Different levels of the organization are thus represented, although no one is included with his immediate superior. The teams undertake intensive problem-solving activities and evaluate their own performance. The focus of the exercises is on developing open and effective group interactions. In phases 3, 4, 5, and 6, these skills and attitudes are extended throughout the organization. Group relations play an important part in the grid approach because of the central role of small groups in both the training and implementation phases. The small group setting provides an important mechanism for unfreezing old attitudes and introducing new ones. The processes are similar to those which are sometimes used in sensitivity training.

The Shell Company of Australia implemented the Managerial Grid as part of its organization development programme.[2] It was initially introduced at the Geelong refinery on the initiative of senior management and personnel staff in order to improve managerial effectiveness, teamwork, and co-operation. The refinery was considered to be a particularly suitable location, as its work force comprised fairly small and cohesive groups of people drawn from a similar social and geographical environment. The company concentrated on the first two phases of the programme. Phase 2 seminars were attended by national groups of management and supervisory staff and concentrated on issues such as communication, co-operation, problem-solving, creativity, and productivity. On the basis of discussions, each team set goals and made plans for improvement in areas it had identified as weak. Evaluation of the programme indicated substantial financial savings and significant improvements in teamwork, planning, and decision-making.

Another company that embarked on teamwork development using the Managerial Grid was Australian Wire Industries.[3] Laboratory-seminar training was held for line and staff personnel at various wire mills in different parts of the country. The seminar was generally given to people considered most likely to be able to influence the effectiveness of the organization. While no quantitative assessment of the success of the programme was made, participants indicated that it opened up communication channels in the organization. People became more concerned about work problems and appeared to exhibit greater commitment to organizational goals. Furthermore, greater co-operation within work groups was evident after the programme was introduced, and people appeared to relate to each other more effectively.

Critics of the Managerial Grid approach have argued that it makes some highly debatable assumptions about human behaviour and conduct. In some cases, proponents of the grid approach tend to advocate a simple, all-purpose leadership style, irrespective of the situational context. Several writers have also pointed to the difficulty of validating claims for the organizational success of the grid approach. In some cases, the numbers of subjects involved in the programme were insufficient to permit scientific verification of the results. In other cases, commentators noted that the grid approach has simply pushed an organization further in the direction in which it was already leading.[4] In one instance, the team-building aspect of the grid programme was so successful in developing a cohesive and united group among the supervisors that the rest of the organization suffered! In another organization where the grid approach was introduced, a number of employees reported that they were left feeling vulnerable and defenceless after they responded openly to attitude questionnaires which asked them to ventilate their feelings about themselves and others. Other employees also claimed that they were ostracized or discriminated against by management when they expressed their disagreement with the philosophical approach underlying the grid.[5]

Proponents of the grid approach stress its general applicability to a wide range of managers in diverse organizational fields. Blake and Mouton claim that their approach has been successfully used throughout the world in production, sales, and R & D departments of private corporations, military, government, welfare, and trade union organizations. Moreover, it has been applied from supervisory jobs to senior executive levels. The six phases of Blake and Mouton's organization development programme also provide a relatively easy and uncomplicated process for organizations to follow. Blake and Mouton have established a world-wide consulting organization known as Scientific Methods, from which firms can obtain assistance when introducing a grid programme. This raises the further problem, however, that organizations may seek to adopt a "standard package" approach to their problems without taking their individual circumstances into account.

The following case study from the mining industry in Australia provides an example of the application of the grid approach to organization development, involving employees at all levels in the enterprise. An interesting aspect of the case is that the grid programme was introduced at the same time as the company was adopting a new approach to industrial relations. The company decided that, as far as possible, supervisors were to be given direct responsibility for industrial relations matters at the shop-floor level. Team building, through the Managerial Grid, was adopted as a means of assisting the process of changing the supervisor's role in the organization.

Case 3: Mount Newman Mining Company

Iron ore accounts for approximately 10 per cent of Australia's annual export income. Almost 90 per cent of the ore is mined in the Pilbara, an area spanning about 200,000 square kilometres in the sparsely populated north-west of Western Australia. The Pilbara iron ore industry consists of ten operating centres with small populations, each isolated from the others. Four large corporations control six open-cut mine sites and four ports. The mines vary in size from approximately one thousand employees at the smallest site to four thousand at the largest. Many of the mine workers are young, single men who come to the Pilbara for a short period to earn high wages and then leave. Annual labour turnover among single men working in the Pilbara is approximately 60 per cent. Workers are mainly employed on shift work, and payment is on a time basis. The mining operations are conducted with large-scale capital equipment under conditions of extreme heat combined with dust and dirt. Earnings are considerably higher than the national average.

Iron ore operations began in the Pilbara in 1966 with Hamersley Iron Pty Ltd commissioning an open-cut mine at Mount Tom Price and port facilities at Dampier. Goldsworthy Mining Limited began operations later that year. The period 1966–71 was one of considerable growth for the industry, with both of the original companies rapidly expanding output. During 1969 a third company, the Mount Newman Mining Co. Ltd, began production with an integrated operation of similar size and scope to that of Hamersley. The demand for labour to build and operate the mines was high and not readily available. Staff employees are non-unionized, but a closed shop operates with regard to manual workers. Nine unions have coverage of the miners, four of which cover 85 per cent of the manual labour force. The largest is the Australian Workers' Union (AWU), which represents 47 per cent of the labour force in the Pilbara.

Industrial Relations in the Pilbara

During the 1970s, the Pilbara was the focus of considerable industrial unrest and strike activity. In 1976 the Pilbara experienced 48.9 stoppages per 1,000 employees compared with a mere 1.9 for the remaining iron-ore and non-coaling mining sectors. Industrial unrest became endemic in the Pilbara during the 1970s. Between 1974 and 1976 estimated stoppages in the Pilbara increased by 52 per cent, while man-hours lost owing to strikes rose by 83 per cent. In order to interpret the pattern of industrial relations in the Pilbara, however, it is useful to distinguish between the period up to 1971, when the industry operated under award conditions, and the period since 1971 which has been characterized by collective agreements between the unions and the mining companies.

At the start of mining operations in 1966, Hamersley and Goldsworthy combined through the Western Australian Employers' Federation and served logs of claims on the unions which led to an award. Between 1966 and 1971 the industry was governed by an award which specified minimum rates of pay and conditions. During this period, however, the site workers gained a strong market position, and on-site work-group bargaining yielded substantial over-award payments. As a result of their successful bargaining with the employers, regional committees representing the interests of all unionists at each site were established. The site organizations became known as the Combined Union Committees (CUCs), and they resisted attempts by the Trades and Labour Council of Western Australia to formalize and control them. Although the CUCs eventually won recognition from the Trades and Labour Council, it was several years before the mining companies were prepared to recognize or accept them.

During the 1970s, industrial relations in the Pilbara became increasingly turbulent and fragmented. After the expiration of the Iron Ore Production and Processing Award in January 1972, the united front which the mining companies had previously maintained in negotiations with the unions broke down and a series of separate industrial agreements were negotiated. In 1972, Hamersley broke ranks when it reached a settlement with the unions outside the limits previously agreed by the companies. This incident set a new negotiating structure for the industry which has persisted ever since. The other companies subsequently followed Hamersley and achieved separate agreements with the unions. The renegotiation of agreements in 1974/75 and 1976/77 was marked by protracted industrial disputation.

Various factors have influenced the high level of industrial unrest in the Pilbara. Firstly, the harsh conditions and isolation of the Pilbara region have provided an environment in which tension is likely to develop. Secondly, the high demand for labour and its scarcity have given workers a strong bargaining position. Thirdly, the hitherto favourable market position of the iron-ore industry enabled the employers to concede high wage increases. Fourthly, the development of strong, independent union structures at each mining site, in the form of the CUCs, has also contributed to the fragmented nature of industrial relations in the Pilbara. At times, the CUCs have tended to formulate their own strategies and take industrial action with little reference to the state branches of the unions involved. The pattern of conflict in the Pilbara reflects the organizational weakness of trade unions at the workplace level. Fifthly, the actions of the employers have also contributed to industrial unrest in the Pilbara. They have been divided in their basic attitudes to industrial relations, fiercely competitive in their demand for labour, and locked into tight delivery schedules and capital servicing. Decisions concerning industrial relations have often been made by head office management who are remote from the mining sites. Furthermore, in many companies little attention has been given to training first-line managers at the site level in order to improve the handling of industrial relations problems.

Background to the Mount Newman Mining Company

The Mount Newman Mining Company is a wholly owned subsidiary of the Broken Hill Proprietary Co. Ltd (BHP). Since 1969, the company has operated the world's largest single open-pit iron ore mine at Mount Whaleback, Newman, in Western Australia. The Mount Whaleback project, which is known as the Mount Newman Joint Venture, includes a number of partners such as the AMAX Iron Ore Corporation of the United States, CSR Limited of Australia, and Mitsui and Co. Ltd of Japan. As well as the open-pit mine at Mount Whaleback, the Mount Newman Joint Venture includes a 426-kilometre railway to Port Hedland, where the ore is unloaded, crushed, stockpiled, and shipped. In 1976 a second ore-handling plant was commissioned at Port Hedland, lifting annual production and shipping capacity to more than forty million tonnes and a total investment in the project to $735 million. By 1978, Mount Newman employed 3,610 people, of whom 1,688 were at Mount Whaleback, 1,521 were at Port Hedland, and 401 were at its Perth office. Forty nationalities were represented in the labour force, of whom 55 per cent were Australian-born.

As shown in table 8, the Mount Newman Joint Venture averaged more man-days lost due to industrial disputes during the period 1972–77 than any other operation in the Pilbara. The worst period of industrial conflict was in 1977, when a dispute at Mount Whaleback eventually forced the entire operation to close. Following a conference before the Western Australian Industrial Commission, Mount Newman decided to conduct their own negotiations with the mining unions. This decision also forced Hamersley and Goldsworthy into separate negotiations which resulted in registered agreements. Negotiations between Mount Newman and the mining unions failed to achieve a settlement, and after renewed industrial action the dispute was referred to the commission for arbitration. Mount Newman thus became the first company in Pilbara to revert to an award.

Organization Development at the Mount Newman
Mining Company

Following the debacle of 1977, Mount Newman decided to adopt a new approach to managing the company. One of the first changes was to transfer the company's head office from

Table 8 Summary of man-days lost in the Pilbara owing to industrial disputes

	1971	1972	1973	1974	1975	1976	1977	1978
Newman								
Newman	n.a.	n.a.	22,173	12,763	21,395	30,815	50,734	2,594
Pt Hedland	n.a.	n.a.	25,164	7,132	8,730	32,350	36,062	1,293
Total	3,730	32,154	47,337	19,895	30,125	63,165	86,796	3,887
Hamersley								
Tom Price	n.a.	n.a.	3,019	2,165	2,221	4,507	3,196	4,615
Paraburdoo	n.a.	n.a.	8,242	3,282	2,019	2,569	3,923	7,800
Dampier	n.a.	n.a.	10,926	5,879	2,758	16,858	7,308	849
Total	6,944	4,718	22,187	11,326	6,998	23,961	14,427	13,264
Goldsworthy								
Goldsworthy	n.a.	n.a.	1,420	2,745	8,516	1,319	2,722	3,380
Shay Gap	n.a.	n.a.	1,208	891	3,760	2,571	5,082	4,438
Finucane	n.a.	n.a.	1,270	1,990	1,097	2,232	3,459	2,394
Total	3,112	1,443	3,898	5,626	13,373	6,122	11,263	10,212
Cliffs								
Pannawanier	n.a.	n.a.	748	1,868	1,913	2,778	1,041	666
Cape Lambert	n.a.	n.a.	4,398	4,155	9,935	6,700	4,529	5,406
Total			5,146	6,023	11,848	9,478	5,570	6,072
Total Pilbara	13,786	38,371	78,568	42,870	62,344	102,728	118,056	33,435
Total W.A.	48,315	94,330	138,083	136,817	131,772	226,978	200,520	71,266

Source: Annual Reports of the Western Australian Industrial Commission.
Note: These reports only include stoppages involving approximately one day or more.

Perth to Port Hedland. By 1979, the number of employees based in Perth had been reduced from approximately 400 to less than 150. The company also embarked on a long-term organization development programme. As shown in figure 14, this programme comprised a number of different components which were designed to improve relationships between the employees and management. In a report to employees in the *Mount Newman Chronicle* of April 1979, the general manager of Mount Newman Mining Company, Irwin Newman, made the following comments:

> The past 12 months have seen the Mt. Newman Mining Company produce and ship more iron ore than in the previous nine years that we have been in business — just over 32 million tons. . . .
>
> A record year is a tribute to our technology, all our people's expertise and the experience which we have built up over 10 years. It shows that we have learned to do many things right and all our people are to be congratulated.
>
> However, we have not got the "people bit" quite right yet and since the future success of the operation relies on the wholehearted support of all Mt. Newman people, I am sure that we must work hard at building a sound "people" base where everybody in the company has respect for himself and the others with whom he works. . . .
>
> I would like to think that with improved communication and a change in management styles and prevailing attitudes, people who work for Mt. Newman will get the type of satisfaction and rewards they would hope for if they were self employed.

Responsibility for introducing the organization development programme lay with Chris Mitchell, development manager for Mount Newman. Mitchell co-ordinated the planning of mineral development as well as organization development at Mount Newman. The background to the new programme was explained by Mitchell as follows:

> What we are putting forward here has to come because, as society changes, so do the requirements of management. Society has changed a great deal over the past 15 years, and management styles just haven't kept pace.
>
> The situation has arisen where people treat each other with suspicion because we don't communicate properly, either as people or departments. If the present exercise succeeds in kicking unfounded suspicions and the "grapevine" out the door, we're half way home.
>
> The aim is to reach the stage where people can trust each other because

Gantt chart — Schedule 1979–1980

No.	ITEM	COMPLETED DATE
1	**INTRODUCTION OF NEW POLICIES**	
	— FEEDBACK IR SAFETY, TRAINING TO EMPLOYEES WITH REASONS FOR CHANGE	24/4
	— IMPLEMENTATION PHASE OF IR SAFETY, TRAINING	END AUG
	— INTRODUCE STAFF POLICIES	5/4
	— PERSONNEL T/T REVIEW OF STAFF POLICIES	10/4
	— FEEDBACK STAFF POLICIES	END JUNE
2	**PLANNING MEETINGS**	
	— INTRODUCE PILOT PROGRAMME	23/8
	— INTRODUCE FULL PROGRAMME	14/12
3	**IR TRAINING PROGRAMME**	
	— PILOT ORIENTATION DAY	23/3
	— FIRST SEMINAR	17-20/4
	— IMPLEMENTATION THROUGH WORKFORCE	JUNE 1980
4	**MANAGERIAL GRID**	
	— REINTRODUCE PHASE 1	MID SEPT
	— REINTRODUCE SUPERVISORY GRID	END NOV
	— REVISE PREVIOUS FRIDAY TASKS	12/6
5	**PLANNING**	
	— CONFIRM SUPERVISORS OBJECTIVES	END APRIL
	— DETERMINE INFORMATION NEEDS OF SUPT/SUPERV.	END MAY
	— DETERMINE INFORMATION NEEDS OF WORKFORCE	22/6
	— DETERMINE OVERALL MGMNT REPORTING SYST.	25/7
	— REVIEW AND APPROVE AREA 3 YEAR PLANS	22/6
	— REVIEW AND APPROVE 10 YEAR PLANS	7/8
6	**TRAINING**	
	— ASSESS LEADERSHIP COURSE AT NEWMAN	10/5
	— ASSESS I/C COURSE AT PORT HEDLAND	20/4
	— INTRODUCE APPROPRIATE LEADERSHIP & I/C COURSE	CONTINUOUS

Legend: MEETING ▶ · ORIGINAL SCHEDULE · ACTUAL PROGRESS

Timeline columns: 1979 — JAN, FEB, MAR, APR, MAY, JUNE, JULY, AUG, SEPT, OCT, NOV, DEC; 1980 — JAN, FEB, MAR, APR, MAY, JUNE they realize they are all working with a common purpose in mind. However, people can't ask just to develop trust. They must be given visible evidence that their newly-developed trust is well placed. This will be a gradual process and is not something that we can expect to occur overnight.

The need for an organization development programme was identified by consultants following extensive work within all departments in the company. The programme involved three basic elements:

1. *Structural aspects*, including the introduction of new formal guidelines and procedures, rules and regulations, budgeting methods or a new organization chart
2. *Technological aspects*, including rearranging the work flow with new physical layouts, work methods, standards, realistic job descriptions, etc.
3. *People aspects*, attempting to develop new attitudes and improving techniques in selection procedures, performance appraisals, and the provision of new training programmes.

The Diagnosis of Problems in the Mount Newman Mining Company

A large number of employees at Mount Newman have attended phase 1 of the Managerial Grid programme, as described earlier. Some of the major problems highlighted by employees at Mount Newman who participated in the grid course were as follows:

1. There was widespread dissatisfaction with management, who were seen as remote and isolated from the employees. There was also little knowledge of company policy devised by management.
2. Employees were dissatisfied with the flow of information on company developments and decisions, particularly on industrial matters. Around 70 per cent of employees reported that the grapevine was their main source of satisfaction.
3. There were insufficient meetings to discuss and plan work. Few bosses appeared to welcome ideas that were not their own. Employees sought recognition for their ideas, even if they were subsequently shown to be misdirected.

4. Employees felt insufficient effort was made to identify and take action on issues affecting their work. Little action was taken on suggestions made by employees.
5. A system was sought which would enable regular assessment to be made of employees and advice given to people on their progress. Less than 50 per cent of employees felt that promotions were given to those who earned them.
6. There was little respect for supervisors among the employees. It was felt that foreman failed to lead people towards greater efforts — mainly because they were the "meat in the sandwich" between management and the shop floor.

The Managerial Grid was introduced by the company as one attempt to reduce barriers between people at different hierarchical levels in the company. It was also seen as a mechanism for enabling employees to gain a better understanding of themselves and others and to assist them to realize the advantages of teamwork compared with individual decision-making. It was hoped that the grid would encourage people to carry the team process through the shop floor.

Industrial Relations and Organization Development

As a result of crises of 1977, Mount Newman reassessed its approach to industrial relations. There were some major changes in the personnel responsible for the industrial relations function in the company. The industrial relations manager subsequently left Mount Newman and joined another mining company. Various task forces were established to inquire into specific problems confronting Mount Newman, such as industrial relations, and to make recommendations concerning required changes. One of the decisions made as a result of this process was to decentralize responsibility for industrial relations decisions to the first-line manager. General policy on industrial relations would continue to be decided by higher-level management, but greater flexibility would be given to supervisors in the way that policy was applied at the workplace level. Correspondingly, supervisors would be held responsible for the decisions they made on industrial relations matters. In order to assist supervisors to become more effective in this area, the company introduced an extensive training programme in industrial relations.

Keeping within its organization development framework, the company sought to involve a wide range of people in the design of a new industrial relations training programme. The task force on industrial relations comprised a "diagonal slice" of people at all three levels from personnel, finance, administration, and the three line areas of mine, railroad, and port. The group took into account many of the comments made by shop floor employees on the new industrial relations policy when drawing up the training programme. The intention was to have the entire Mount Newman work force attend the industrial relations programme in area teams over a twelve-month period. The objectives of the programme were:

1. To allow everyone to gain a better understanding of some of the rules, regulations, awards and agreements presently in force
2. To discuss with their supervisors, and other people attending, what decisions they would make under certain circumstances
3. To enable people to understand the attitudes they have developed personally, compared with the attitudes necessary to successfully handle work situations.

The Impact of Organizational Changes at Mount Newman on the Supervisor's Role

Considerable emphasis has been given in the organization development programme to upgrading the competence of the first-line manager. At the same time it has been stressed that the long-term aim of the programme is to enlarge the job of shop-floor workers so that close supervision is no longer required. The potential conflict between these objectives is apparent in the following statement made by the company in the *Mount Newman Chronicle*:

It is appreciated that many supervisors and foremen will feel ill at ease with this new policy, and the training programme is directly aimed at providing them with more confidence and knowledge in handling the problems . . .

Undoubtedly a change in management style will hit snags. One will be resistance from employees. Some will not be interested in more challenging jobs; some jobs may not lend themselves to enrichment. A major barrier is also likely to be management attitude and management resistance. . . .

As people take on more responsibility, less supervision is needed — and that supervision relies more on all-round participation. This alone can make many staff members feel threatened.

In order to improve the status of the first-line manager, the company introduced a new salary scale for supervisory-level staff which improved their relative position. Nevertheless, technological changes are seen by many supervisors as a threat to their job security and career prospects. At Port Hedland, for example, a new computerized crushing and distribution plant requires only two operators — compared with the seventy operators and supervisors that were needed to achieve a similar level of production in the old plant. An attempt by the company to improve career opportunities for its supervisory and other staff has been to offer them opportunities to apply for positions in the larger BHP organization. This has also meant, however, that BHP staff are now able to apply for jobs in Mount Newman.

While many of the innovations introduced by the Mount Newman Mining Company should assist it to anticipate future events more easily and to develop better employee relations in some areas, long-term difficulties exist with regard to the industry as a whole. Many of the factors identified as contributing to industrial relations problems in the Pilbara are endemic to isolated mining ventures and have been exacerbated by actions taken by the mining companies in the past.

The organization development programme developed by Mount Newman may assist in ameliorating some aspects of relations between labour and management, but it is unlikely to have major impact on the fundamental problems of industrial relations confronting the company. The future role of the supervisor will be determined largely by economic and technological changes in the industry.

6

The Group Technology Approach

Most of Australian manufacturing is composed of what are commonly called "job shops" — manufacturing operations using a collection of conventional machines and equipment and producing small batches of product (typically, anything up to a couple of hundred units) in response to specific customer orders. The remainder of Australian manufacturing can conveniently be categorized into continuous-flow, assembly-line, and project operations. An oil refinery is an example of a continuous flow production process, car manufacture involves the archetypal assembly line, and building a ship is an example of project-type manufacture.

Assembly or fabrication lines are machine paced, which result in highly repetitive and often boring and monotonous work. In addition, these lines involve large capital investment. So it is not surprising that most public attention has been directed to this form of manufacture (see chap. 7). But despite this, it is batch manufacture in job shops which is the dominant form of manufacture (for example, it constitutes 35 per cent of America's manufacturing base[1] and 60 per cent of Britain's manufacturing labour force[2]) and which provides the greatest potential for productivity gains (for example, only about 5 per cent of the total time required to produce any part is spent in actual metal cutting in a traditional job shop).

This chapter concentrates on batch manufacture in Australia, examines some of the system changes that are occurring (with particular emphasis on group technology) and which will occur in the future (for example, computer-aided manufacture), and details the impact of these changes on the first-line manager. Two case studies — Mulgrave Gear and Ajax Pumps — are included in the chapter as examples of the current rate of change occurring in Australia in this area.

Group Technology

Group technology reduces the cost of producing small lots of parts by making small-lot production more like mass production. It does this by organizing parts and machines into groups so that several small lots can be manufactured together in a larger lot. Group technology is applied to a small-lot manufacturing situation by a combination of a parts classification scheme and physically regrouping machines on the job shop floor.

At the moment, most small-lot manufacturing is done in job shops using a functional plant layout similar to that shown in figure 15. Here machines are grouped by type or process; lathes, mills, grinders, and drills, for example, are grouped near

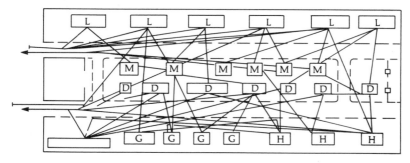

Key: L = lathe
        M = milling machine
        G = grinder
        D = drill
        H = hobber

(Reproduced, by permission, from Burbidge, *Introduction of Group Technology*, p. 4.)

Figure 15 Functional plant layout

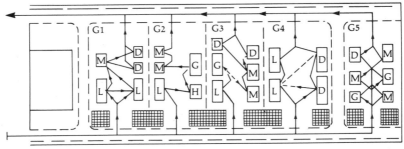

Key: L = lathe
        M = milling machine
        G = grinder
        D = drill
        H = hobber

(Reproduced, by permission, from Burbidge, *Introduction of Group Technology*, p. 4.)

Figure 16   Group plant layout

other lathes, mills, grinders, or drills. Any part requiring multiple machine operation must move relatively long distances between machine centres. If, instead, machines are grouped together on the basis of the families of parts which will use a particular combination of machines, then progress has been made towards the economies inherent in mass production. This machine regrouping can be done in one of two basic ways: (1) different machines can be grouped together into work cells, as is shown in figure 16, or (2) a series of flow lines can be established, as shown in figure 17. In either case specialization is based on components, with one flow line or group being established for each family of parts as against the functional layout where process specialization is achieved. The group layout is more flexible than the flow-line layout, as there is no need to restrict the sequence of machine usage within any machine group — for the flow line the families of machines are always used in the same flow sequence.

The second essential component of group technology is a parts classification scheme. An effective parts classification scheme makes the task of establishing parts families to move through the machine cells or flow lines much easier. Classifica-

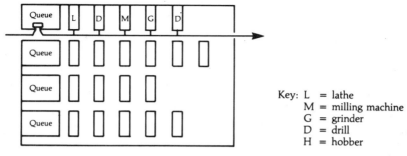

Key: L = lathe
M = milling machine
G = grinder
D = drill
H = hobber

(Reproduced, by permission, from Burbidge, *The Introduction of Group Technology*, p. 3.)

Figure 17   Flow-line plant layout

tion schemes can be divided into those which are based on a parts design feature (graphic classification) and those which are based on manufacturing attributes (manufacturing-oriented classification).[3] The main shape of the part, the number, location, and shape of holes, slots, flats, and threads — information that can be found on the engineering drawing of the part — are used for graphics classification, while manufacturing-oriented classification requires additional information such as processing data, lot size, routings, and standard cost data.

Once a satisfactory parts classification scheme has been established, the next requirement for any company wishing to set up a group technology structure is to create appropriate groupings of machines. These groupings should be such that the processing and scheduling of parts is efficient without creating undue excess capacity. Burbidge[4] has proposed a method of doing this based on present part routings rather than part design or shape characteristics. This method is called *product flow analysis* and involves three levels of analysis: grouping factory processes and their parts into departments; grouping each department's machines and establishing families for the department's parts; and sequencing of the department's machines to achieve a flow line.

Table 9 Typical job design — group technology and traditional batch manufacture

Desirable Job Features	Positive Features of Group Technology	Negative Features of Group Technology	Traditional Batch Production
Task identity/significance	Completion of whole components within groups enables a degree of task identity. (*Inherent in GT.*)	Manufacture based on components compared with whole products.	Task identity very low — not even a whole component is completed in functional groups or by individuals.
Task variety	Variety facilitated by multi-skilling and job rotation within and between cell groups. (*Optional for GT.*)	Individuals' variety determined by the machine(s) they control and component design of a single family of similar components. Aim of GT is to reduce variation at each machine to facilitate reduced resetting.	Individuals' variety determined by machine(s) they control and component design of total range of components — multi-skilling and rotation between functional groups is possible.
Autonomy: Group	a. Factory production and control is simplified due to the cell structure. Within the limits of the production cycle, planning and control of manufacture in each cell group therefore can be left to the group members. (*Optional for GT.*)	The shorter the production cycle (an aim of GT being to reduce that cycle length), the less the degree of discretion available to the cell groups to control and plan manufacture.	Doubtful that any form of group working within the framework of functional layout could achieve autonomy in planning and control because of factory-wide complexities.
	b. Cell groupings are self-contained and are independent of other cell groupings in terms of their production. (*Inherent in GT.*)	Because manufacture is component based (with distinction between machine cells, assembly, fabrication quality control, stores etc.) a degree of centralised control is required to co-ordinate product manufacture.	Functional groups are inter-dependent in terms of their production. Their degree of independence is largely dependent on the presence of buffer stocks.
	c. The group structure enables greater participation and autonomy in wider issues, e.g. leadership, work hours, selection etc. (*Optional for GT.*)		Whilst an effective form of group working enabling autonomy (in issues such as leadership, work hours etc.) could be achieved, the lack of task interdependence in a functional group would restrict group identity, cohesion.
Autonomy: Individual	Work pace and freedom largely dependent on group decision (if sufficient autonomy given). (*Optional for GT.*)	Reduced buffer stocks and the objective to operate key machine(s) continuously may result in the machine pacing of operators, giving them less freedom. Increased systemisation of production must [...]	Work pace and freedom largely dependent on the supervisor.

Table 9 (cont'd) Typical job design — group technology and traditional batch manufacture

Desirable Job Features	Positive Features of Group Technology	Negative Features of Group Technology	Traditional Batch Production
Challenge	Opportunity for growth and new skills depends on optional multi-skilling, rotation and group autonomy in planning and control. (*Optional for GT.*)	Reduced need for the complex skill of machine resetting.	Opportunity for growth and new skills depends on optional multi-skilling and rotation.
Social support	a. Cell group structure and operator interdependence promote development of supportive friendships, feedback and group identity. (*Inherent in GT.*)	Cell group composition in terms of: • no. of machines and types • no. of operators and skills • physical layout is determined by technical requirements. Because people accompany machines, a rearrangement may group together individuals who are incompatible or hinder existing social patterns, leading to social conflict.	Functional groups provide social support, but lack of operator interdependence restricts group identity and cohesion.
	b. Each operator is more closely identified with his work quality within the cell group; greater opportunity for recognition. (*Inherent in GT.*)		Because an operator in a functional group partly completes a component, which then goes on to another functional group, little feedback and recognition for quality work can be achieved.
Desirable future	a. If optional multi-skilling, rotation, group autonomy are carried out, operators will have a wider range of skills to master and will generally be more employable within and outside the company. (*Optional for GT.*)	Reduced number of skilled setters and progress chasers reduce opportunity generally.	Setters etc. required. Optional multi-skilling, rotation enhance prospects.
	b. System of GT is more productive/efficient, therefore less chance of company failure or redundancy. (*Inherent in GT.*)		The low efficiency of functional layout may lead to cutbacks in staff to reduce costs.

Source: Stiller, "Group Technology — Maximizing its Benefits Through Job Design", pp. 24-25.

The First-Line Manager and Group Technology

With a traditional batch manufacturing process, each operator will load, tend, and unload a specific machine. With group technology (GT), a number of operators will typically work together in a GT cell tending a group of disparate machines. Naturally, the characteristics of the job will be substantially different. Stiller has developed a comparative chart, reproduced in table 9, which highlights the job design differences between group technology and traditional batch manufacture.[5] From this comparison he makes these points:

1. Autonomy in production planning and control for operators in a GT environment is possible, but is usually quite limited.
2. Significant benefits can occur for the operators, such as (a) increased autonomy and control over their work; (b) increased social support, teamwork, and recognition; (c) greater task identity. But disadvantages also can occur — namely, reduced skill owing to less frequent machine resetting, and reductions and redeployment of the work force generally.
3. GT offers greater opportunities for group working, multiskilling, job rotation, autonomy, and participation than does traditional batch production.

But where does the introduction of group technology leave the first-line manager? To a large degree the responsibility for planning and controlling the GT cell production will move to a higher level of management (typically a staff manufacturing person or group) or to the operators in the cell itself. The size of each production "run" and the "load" to be placed on each GT cell at the beginning of each planning period/production cycle is likely to be determined at a level higher than the first-line manager. Detailed scheduling may well become the province of the cell operators. This leaves the first-line manager with the role of a "resource person" — to anticipate and meet the physical and informational requirements of his operators.

An Evaluation of Group Technology

From an operations management viewpoint, a group technology structure has three primary benefits over a functional layout for a job shop:

1. A reduction in machine set-up time
2. A reduction in work-in-process inventories
3. A reduction in materials handling costs

These cost savings were achieved by both organizations described in the case studies to follow — Mulgrave Gear and Ajax Pumps.

But group technology has not been adopted by industry to any great degree owing to some practical difficulties associated with introducing GT. These are highlighted in table 10, which contains a list of many of the features that distinguish a manufacturing environment suitable for group technology. The "ideal" situation, as gathered from the literature and from industry,[6] is shown in the first column of the table, followed in the second column by the response of a survey of UK organizations using group technology.[7] The remainder of the table shows the situation at Mulgrave Gear and Ajax Pumps. Two points of interest emerge from the table. The first is the relative under-utilization of machines, and the second is the lower than expected level of worker participation in the "management" of the cell. Management should be aware of the likelihood of machine under-utilization before group technology cells are planned — the important point is to follow Ajax Pumps' lead and ensure that the under-utilized machines are not the most expensive ones. If a company is looking towards group technology as a means of increasing worker participation, caution should be exercised because this has not been a primary benefit in the experience of others.

Undue emphasis on classification schemes also appears to be a block to the effective introduction of group technology. If classification of all parts is attempted, the problem of what to do with the residual parts that do not fit neatly into family classifications always remains. Ajax Pumps and Mulgrave Gear have both been successful with group technology because they

Table 10 Features of group technology manufacture

	Ideal*	Average of UK Industry†	Mulgrave Gear's Sprocket Line	Ajax Pumps' Impeller Cell
Operational characteristics:				
Ratio of machines to men	Not important	1.3 to 1	3 to 1	3 to 1
Work completed outside the cell (%)	0	"small amount"	35	2
Other work coming into the cell (%)	0	74% of responding firms had some work coming in	40	5
Variation of work within the cell	Not important	20% very varied 32% varied 16% similar 32% very similar	Very similar	Very similar
Average batch size	Not important	330	450	30
Operators doing more than two jobs (%)	100	78	100	100
Groups store own drawings and tools	Yes	70% yes	Yes	No
Men move occasionally into or out of cell	No	Yes	Yes	Yes
Cell physically separated from rest of job shop	Yes-essential	90% yes	Yes	Yes
Decentralization of responsibility:				
Groups responsible for own inspection	Yes	75% yes	Yes	Yes
Groups responsible for processing own work	Yes	89% yes	Yes	Yes
Operators move of own accord	Probably	33% yes	No	No
Group members participate in selection of new staff	Possibly	7% yes	No	No
Groups established for employee training and development	Yes	No	No	No
Group leader elected by group	Possibly	No	No	No
Classification scheme used	—	46% formal 24% "natural" 17% experience 13% product flow analysis	Product flow analysis	Natural classification and product flow analysis
Top management commitment to group technology	Yes	Yes in successful groups	Yes	Yes

Table adapted from an internal company report, prepared by B.J. Dempster at Ajax Pumps.
* Source: B.J. Dempster, Ajax Pumps; Burbidge, *The Introduction of Group Technology*; Gallagher and Knight, *Group Technology*.
† Source: "A Survey of Cellular Manufacturing Cells".

have initially set up cells with parts that make sense from a practical point of view — experience rather than a formalized classification scheme provides the direction to follow. As additional cells are considered, the effect on the operation of the residual part of the job shop is evaluated before any action is taken.

The Future

Most group technology has been implemented using traditional machines or grouping traditional machines around a machine with numerical control. Numerical control (NC) is usually applied to milling and other metal-cutting operations using as a control a punched paper tape. As design changes only require changing the paper tape, the NC machine provides manufacturing flexibility as well as increased accuracy and uniformity. With current technology, microcomputers are much more effective as the medium of control than paper tape. Nor need the microcomputer be limited to the control of a single machine. Computer-aided design (CAD) and computer-aided manufacturing (CAM) provide the inevitable future for batch manufacturing.[8] CAM will be used to control a series of machine centres which constitute a facility now being called a flexible manufacturing system. With this type of system, the work group can be responsible for loading, monitoring, unloading, routine repairs, and tool-setting. Planning and control will probably be the responsibility of a central staff section. The role of the supervisor will still be that of a "resource person".

Case 4: Mulgrave Gear

The Mulgrave Gear Company manufactures and distributes over twenty thousand products, most of which are related to the transmission and control of speed and power. Of the products sold by Mulgrave Gear, approximately 40 per cent are resale items. Manufactured products include gears, sprockets, cylinders, universal joints, and couplings. Most manufacturing operations performed involve metal cutting or other metal-forming operations from such raw materials as castings or steel bars.

In recent years Mulgrave Gear has set up nearly a quarter of its manufacturing volume in a work-cell or machine-centre structure. While the company has experienced several disadvantages with this type of structure, there have been significant advantages and the net experience has been favourable. Mulgrave Gear plans to push ahead with further applications of the work-cell or group-technology structure over the next few years although it realizes that nowhere near all their manufacturing operations can be converted.

Before they had even set up the first work cell Mulgrave Gear felt that they would have a union problem. As Carl Van Etten, the manufacturing manager, recalled, the union "knew right away it was job erosion". Mulgrave Gear operates a bidding system for jobs, and when the first work cell jobs came up for bid there were no bids. And so, at first, employees with low seniority were forced to work the cells and some new people were hired from outside the company. But in time, when the higher wages earned in the cells became common knowledge, it was not difficult to fill these positions despite the minimal rest time possible when doing this work. Mulgrave Gear historically has had very low turnover rates and absenteeism, which was felt by management to be due to the relatively high wages paid. So it was expected that staffing the highly paid cell jobs would not remain a problem for long.

While staffing was an initial problem, there certainly was another side to this issue. Before the cell structure was introduced, Mulgrave Gear employed 600 on the shop floor, but two years later the figure had fallen to 310 — 200 on the day shift and 110 on the night shift. The number of supervisors needed had remained constant. Even though a cell required less direct time from the foreman, more time was needed for supporting activities such as tool preparation. There were also other advantages in addition to the 30 per cent reduction in direct labour. The ratio of run time to set-up time had increased from 1:1 to 3:1, with set-ups ranging from 7.5 to 10.25 hours.

Work-in-process inventories had been reduced by 35 per cent. In addition, the production manager, Bill Ingles, felt there were now greater feelings of job security, job satisfaction, and satisfaction with the higher wages for those employed in the work cells.

But Mulgrave Gear had found that they needed a large amount of capital equipment to make the new structure work. High capital equipment costs and eroded flexibility were some of the prices to be paid. Speaking of the work cells, Bill Ingles stated that if you "do it too much your capacity goes to pot. It is possible to continue to reduce costs by introducing more and more work cells, but eventually other product lines will be put out of business."

Work cells were established at Mulgrave Gear in two basic ways. Either several machines (on average, three) were grouped to produce a single product, or four or five machines were used for several products in what became known as "multi-machine manning". A typical work cell might contain a saw, a drill, and two auto lathes.

An example of the economic benefits of work cells to Mulgrave Gear is the production of sprockets. Five machines were required (a six-spindle screw machine, two hobbers, a burr and wire bush machine, and a rotary stamping machine) using the previous method of manufacture. One employee operated each of these machines, although one man operated both hobbers. The total time to produce one sprocket was 0.875 minutes. Labour costs were $7.46 per hour plus fringe benefits of 35 per cent, which, for a 2,000-hour working year, is about $20,000 per employee. This labour cost together with materials cost and overhead amounts to a $47 per hour (or $0.783 per minute) cost to produce sprockets. The cost per sprocket is then 0.875 minutes multiplied by $0.783 or $0.68. Using a cell structure, one man can operate the screw machine, one hobber, the burr and wire brush machine, and the stamping machine. He is limited by the 0.43 minutes per sprocket on the hobber, but he can produce one complex sprocket in these 0.43 minutes. The cost of a sprocket using a work cell is then 0.43 minutes multiplied by $0.783 or $0.377. From 68 cents down to 34 cents per sprocket is a 50 per cent cost reduction.

Sometimes duplication of relatively inexpensive machines provides a way of levelling the flow of work through a cell. Change gears at Mulgrave Gear are at present manufactured using an outside diameter turning lathe (replacement cost $20,000), a gear hobber (replacement cost $50,000), and a stamping machine (replacement cost $500). The company is currently considering setting up a work cell containing no lathe, four hobbers and four stampers. A lathe is not needed if the blanks forming the raw material for the work group are of fifteen different forms rather than the ten currently being used. This change will require a $20,000 additional investment in equipment and new patterns. But with the work cell, set-ups will be reduced, one position in the hobbing section of the traditional job shop can be eliminated, and the $20,000 lathe is not needed. In addition, production rates will increase.

Work-cell structure or group technology has been successful at Mulgrave Gear. When internal production costs for couplings could not compete with the costs of overseas manufacture, couplings were obtained from Taiwan. A cell structure brought costs down enough to enable the production of couplings to resume at Mulgrave Gear. Reduced labour costs and work-in-process inventory costs have outweighed the costs of additional capital equipment required. A surprising result is that the expected job enlargement benefits might not have eventuated. Bill Ingles commented: "In a cell structure, the difficulty of the job has decreased because the man is now working on one product rather than many."

Case 5: Ajax Pumps

Group technology started at Ajax Pumps with the aim to rearrange completely the layout of the factory. But this attempt was a failure owing to the difficulty of developing a classification scheme for over four thousand different products. Instead, when a new Heinemann turret lathe was delivered, a group technology cell was developed around this machine by examining the routing sheets for all products that might require machining on the new lathe. This process resulted in a group technology cell being established to manufacture pump impellers — a bronze disc-shaped casting which requires profile turning, drilling, keyway broaching, and dynamic balancing. The impeller cell was established so that the new turret lathe, which was the most expensive machine in the cell, was the bottleneck machine — faster or equivalent throughput was obtainable in all other parts of the cell. First, the bronze casting is turned on each side on the Heinemann auto turret lathe and then another specialized turning operation is performed by the second machine in the cell, a seven-capstan lathe. From here the impeller moves to a broach, where a centre keyway is cut and then to a drill where the central hole is drilled and burnished. Finally, the impeller is tested on the dynamic balancer and balance adjustments made, if needed, using a milling machine. Some impellers produced by Ajax Pumps (about 10 per cent) cannot use this sequence of machines and are still produced in the main job shop. Those impellers produced in the cell travel on specially made trolleys about 6 metres during manufacture as against a movement of 36 metres previously required in the job shop.

In addition to the impeller cell, Ajax has established cells for the manufacture of shafts, casings, and "small rotational components". About 50 per cent of production is done in the group technology cells and the remaining 50 per cent in the main job shop. Barrie Dempster, the production manager at Ajax, believes this is as far as the company can go with group technology: "The rest of the throughput is too variable and the lots are too small for GT."

Ajax has derived the following advantages from the changeover to a group technology method of manufacture:

1. Savings and efficiencies in materials handling. Travel distances have been substantially reduced, and also the machine operators can move the specialized trolleys without the need of materials-handling men or equipment.
2. Production planning is less complex. Only the first machine of a cell has to be loaded.

3. Throughput time has decreased. In the shaft cell, for example, average batch production time has dropped from 6.7 weeks to 3.9 weeks.
4. Work-in-process inventories have dropped, but raw material inventories have increased slightly (to avoid delays in starting a batch in the cells) giving an overall reduction of about 8 per cent.
5. Labour turnover in the group technology areas is approximately one-third of the average turnover for the rest of the plant.
6. Machine operators have become associated with an entire product and not just a single process. This has developed a greater sense of pride in the work.
7. Production of a product comes under the responsibility of a single supervisor, which has resulted in higher quality, better scheduling, and a considerable reduction in the time spent job chasing.

While Ajax Pumps has not reduced its labour force over the period of two to three years during which group technology has been implemented, effective excess capacity has been built up.

The Socio-Technical Systems Approach

Theories of organization behaviour have been radically changed by the development of the systems approach. Many of the basic concepts of systems theory have been derived from the physical and biological sciences. In biology, an organism is regarded as a system of mutually dependent parts, each of which includes various sub-systems. The human body, for instance, has a skeletal system, a circulatory system, and a nervous system, all of which are closely interrelated; hence, a fault in the nervous system is likely to result in circulatory problems. Similarly, an organization is composed of a number of parts or sub-systems which are highly dependent on one another for successful operation. A manufacturing company, for example, consists of a production system, which makes the product, as well as a marketing system, which ensures that the product is sold. The survival of the enterprise depends on the effective integration of each of these systems. The marketing system requires a good product to ensure sales, while the production system is dependent upon effective marketing in order to obtain the capital to produce more.

A detailed application of the systems approach to social structures was first provided by Talcott Parsons,[1] who advanced the notion that organizations have three interrelated levels: the technical or production level, the organizational or managerial level, and the institutional or community level. The technical level is concerned with the actual performance of tasks within the organization. In a business enterprise, this may involve the production of goods and services; in a school, it will be the education of students; in a hospital, the treatment of patients. The organizational level involves the integration of tasks performed by the technical system. A function of management at this level is to integrate the input of material, energy, and information from the technical core. At the institutional level, the organization receives and transforms inputs from the external environment. The organization faces the greatest degree of uncertainty in dealing with environmental inputs over which it has little or no control. It is the role of the general manager to mediate between the institution and the external environment. The interrelationship between the three levels of the organizational system is shown in figure 18.

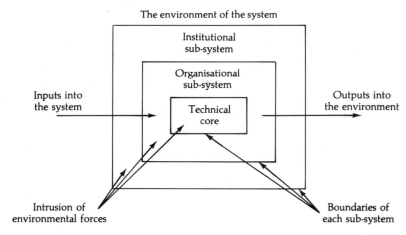

(Reproduced, by permission, from Lansbury and Gilmour, *Organisations: An Australian Perspective*, p. 41.)

Figure 18   The organization as an open system

The Socio-Technical Systems Model

The systems approach has undergone considerable development since Parsons's contribution. In Britain, social scientists at the Tavistock Institute of Human Resources have developed the concept of the socio-technical system.[2] As a result of studies in a variety of industries and countries, the Tavistock researchers concluded that every organization consists of both social and technical sub-systems. The social sub-system is the relationship between the participants in the organization; the technical sub-system consists of the tasks to be performed and includes the relevant equipment, facilities, and techniques. According to A.K. Rice, one of the early Tavistock researchers, "the concept of a socio-technical system arose from the consideration that any production system requires both a technological organization — equipment and process layout — and a work organization relating to each other those who carry out the necessary tasks. The technological demands place limits upon the type of work organization possible, but a work organization has social and psychological properties of its own that are independent of technology."[3] Hence, organizations are not simply technical or social systems, but the structuring of human activities around various technologies. While technology affects the types of inputs and outputs to and from an organization, the social sub-system determines the effectiveness and efficiency of the utilization of the technology.

The socio-technical systems approach to job redesign has given considerable emphasis to the role of the work group. The ideal socio-technical system, in fact, is one in which the technical aspects of the work are organized so that the immediate work group has a meaningful unit of activity, responsibility for its task, and a satisfactory set of interpersonal relationships. A work situation in which tasks are interdependent requires not only job redesign but also team-building. Research has shown that a major weakness in many job-enrichment programmes stems from the fact that they are focused on the individual rather than the group. Sometimes this may mean enriching one individual's job at the cost of reducing another's. Furthermore, where job-enrichment schemes are imposed by management, they lose the motivational energy released through direct participation by employees themselves. Finally, job redesign that takes account of group dynamics and team factors can motivate and enrich the jobs of team members collectively. Research conducted by the Tavistock Institute[4] has identified the following conditions as critical to work groups, both in the achievement of their tasks and in meeting the human needs of their members:

1. *Whole tasks*. A task must be such that those engaged on its parts can experience, as a group, completion of the whole task.

2. *Self regulation*. A group must be able to regulate its own activities and be judged by its results.

3. *Optimum size*. A group must be of such a size that it not only can regulate its own activities but can also provide satisfactory personal relationships.

4. *Optimum skill range*. The group should possess the full range of skills required for the completion of its tasks.

5. *Minimal status differences*. Status should be minimized so that the internal structure of the group remains stable and members are prepared to accept internal leadership.

6. *The development of parallel groups*. A group should not be unique, so that when members of small work groups become dissatisfied, they are able to move to other groups engaged in similar tasks.

The terms *autonomous* or *semi-autonomous* have been used to describe work groups that possess the qualities described above. Work groups may experience varying degrees of autonomy depending on the extent to which the group is able to determine its own goals, work methods, work allocation, work times, leadership, and membership. Within each of these areas there may be a wide range of possibilities. The question of leadership, for example, might be decided by the group acting on its own, in consultation with management, or with management's approval. The context in which the group is working may also influence the degree of autonomy it is able to exercise. In the production field, for example, highly mechanized assembly lines provide little opportunity for worker autonomy in regard to work goals, task allocation, or performance. It is unlikely that the autonomy of a production group would extend to the determination of the product to be made, the establishment of overall production targets, or the amount and method of remuneration. This is not to deny the possibility, however, of a considerably higher degree of autonomy than has been the case under traditional methods of working.

Examples of Socio-Technical Systems of Organization

The operation of semi-autonomous groups may, in fact, best be understood by comparison with the traditional organizational structure of a production section.[5] As shown in figure 19, the

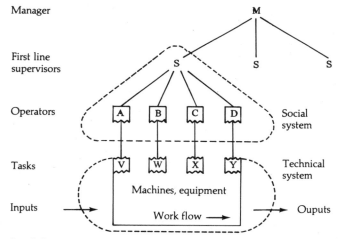

(Reproduced, by permission, from H.W. Peter, "Designing Human Work: A New Challenge", *Work and People* 1, no. 1 [1975]: 6.)

Figure 19   The traditional structure of work organization in the production section of a factory

basic structure of the traditional work system is one worker performing one task per shift. The production section is hierarchically organized around the first-line manager who is responsible for the performance of the section in regard to the quantity and quality of output. The performance goals are set by the manager and given by instruction to the supervisor.

The supervisor has the authority and responsibility for allocating tasks, for co-ordinating interdependent task performance, and for overseeing task performance; he or she is accountable for everything that happens in the section. The workers perform the tasks assigned to them and are usually rewarded on the basis of their specific task performance. They are not expected to know much about what others in their section do, except when this is specified in their job description. To prevent a supervisor from imposing additional work when they are not busy, the workers may develop informal quotas, or dargs, to restrict production norms to what they consider reasonable in relation to the reward system. The goals of the supervisor and his subordinates are separated in the organizational structure. The supervisor's goals are concerned with the overall performance of the section, while the subordinates' goals are limited to the performance of their individual tasks. Communications are essentially a one-way process down the hierarchy, and the workers are given no opportunity to participate in decisions about the section as a whole.

In the semi-autonomous work group system, the basic structural unit is the complete work team. As shown in figure 20, the team is organized around achieving the work group's goals in regard to both task performance (the quality and quantity of work) and human effectiveness (fulfilment of social and psychological needs). These goals are jointly set by the group

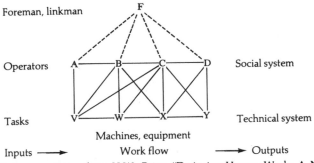

(Reproduced, by permission, from H.W. Peter, "Designing Human Work: A New Challenge", *Work and People* 1, no. 1 [1975]: 6.)

Figure 20 The structure of a semi-autonomous work team in the production section of a factory

members and mangement. Using the symbols shown in figure
20, the team members ABCD take collective responsibility for
allocating the tasks VWXY in the work group. The allocation of
tasks may change depending on the skills required and the
demands of work. The lines connecting the tasks and team
members illustrate the interrelationship of the social and
technical system. The role of the supervisor is no longer simply
one of supervision. He or she now acts as a link between the
work group and management. On behalf of the group, the
supervisor ensures that there is a sufficient input of materials
and that outputs are passed to the users. The supervisor may
also keep records, assist in the selection and training of group
members, and generally provide help to the group as needed. In
short, the supervisor has become a manager of the boundary
conditions of the group, including its relationships with other
groups and long-term planning, enabling the work group to
manage its internal affairs.

Australian Cases

Many examples of the introduction of semi-autonomous work
groups have been recorded in the literature.[6] An Australian
example of the introduction of semi-autonomous work groups
occurred at the Welvic plant of ICI Australia Ltd.[7] The establishment of a new plant at a "greenfields" site provided the opportunity to involve employees in building a new socio-technical
system from its inception. The aim of the new approach was to
develop greater job fulfilment, make better use of capital equipment and raw materials, and achieve a higher level of productivity. The number of employees involved in the new plant was
nine, together with three members of management. The staff
were carefully selected by advertising for people who were
interested in working as part of a team, taking responsibility,
and developing themselves through their work. People with a
wide range of abilities and experience were chosen so that each
shift team would be able to solve complex problems. All were
given extensive training to develop the required skills in
problem-solving and decision-making and to establish a sense of

group cohesion. After consultation between the staff, management, and the unions, a number of new practices were agreed upon. The main changes involved eliminating the position of the supervisor and transferring responsibilities for planning and organizing to operators organized in shift teams. The operators formed themselves into two-person shift teams, in conjunction with the plant superintendent, and made their own arrangements for maintenance, cleaning, interchange of tasks, and shift rosters. The teams were given access to information on plant performance and costs. They were also involved in planning changes in the plant and problem-solving. Regular team-building sessions were conducted to assist the groups in decision-making and co-operative working. The sessions also provided teams with the opportunity to communicate with each other, to obtain refresher training on technical aspects, and to review their performance. The terms of employment for operators were also changed to give them responsibility for maintaining their own time cards, which eliminated supervision of time-keeping.

An issue that needs to be faced by management, however, is the equitable sharing between the employer and employees of the profits gained through increased productivity. One British writer, Ray Wild, has singled out payment systems as the crucial issue affecting the success of job restructuring: "In many cases workers either received or pressed for increases in wages . . . to compensate for their utilisation of further skills, their flexibility or assumption of greater responsibility. Since in many cases the 'introduction of organisational changes led directly to the reduction in supervisory requirements and therefore in the cost of supervision, many companies have been prepared to offer increased financial rewards to workers."[8] This is an important issue which has not yet been fully resolved. The growth of direct bargaining in Australia and elsewhere means that trade unions will certainly press for a share in benefits that ensue.[9]

Evaluating the Socio-Technical Systems Approach

The socio-technical systems approach to the analysis of work and organizations has evolved over a considerable period of time and embraces a wide range of workplace studies. Nevertheless, a number of criticisms have been made of the approach which should be noted. Rose claims that some writers "endow technology with a primary explanatory value" regardless of whether they are examining interplant conflict, managerial effectiveness, or .psychological deprivation.[10] Although sociopsychological attachments of people in the workplace are taken into account by socio-technical systems theorists, they tend to be relegated to secondary importance. Furthermore, economic variables are often ignored, even when these provide the most powerful constraints on organizations and those who work in them. Carey[11] has also criticized the socio-technical systems approach for disregarding the powerful influence of pay and other economic incentives on individuals and work-group behaviour. He attributes the success of some of the examples cited by the Tavistock researchers as being due more to economic variables than the social or technical systems.

Another difficulty with the socio-technical systems approach is the degree to which organizations and other social institutions can be likened to biological organisms. Silverman finds the notion that organizations are living entities with pseudo-biological needs for survival, stability, growth, and so on both absurd and illogical.[12] He claims that the needs or actions often attributed to organizations as entities are often either suspiciously similar to those of organizational leaders or those the researcher or consultant simply believes will improve efficiency. Even if it is conceded that organizations and their behaviour may be understood as a series of adaptations to the surrounding environment, this does not explain why organizations often react in different ways to external or internal threats to their stability. Furthermore, unless the motivations of individual members or groups within an organization are taken into account, it is difficult to explain why organizations possess certain characteristics and behave in a particular way.

In a reappraisal of the socio-technical systems approach, Kelly[13] notes that its theoretical developments have proceeded in two main directions: one that emphasizes individual job design, another concerned more with the significance of the work group. These two approaches tend to conflict with each other. One of the pioneers of the socio-technical systems theory, Fred Emery, has pursued the work-group approach and advocated the development of "self managing groups" within organizations.[14] Emery notes that many of the early Tavistock studies of socio-technical systems were conducted in traditional industrial settings such as coalmining, textiles, and metal fabrication. In each of these settings, the main problem was to ascertain how much autonomy would be consistent with the organization's production plans, maintenance procedures, and so on. In continuously operating plants, such as pulp and paper manufacturing, where the conditions of an open workshop and face-to-face interaction are no longer present, Emery argues for the establishment of self-managing work groups. Such groups undertake all work tasks, including those formerly performed by quality-control engineers and production planners in traditional organizations. Self-managing work groups, however, will require more carefully planned forms of management than previously existed under the *laissez-faire* or authoritarian systems of the past. Emery also notes that management will be required to negotiate agreements with the self-managing groups about their objectives and activities.

The following case studies provide contrasting examples of the socio-technical systems approach. The Volvo plant at Kalmar has been one of the most highly publicized examples of new work organization which has utilized both semi-autonomous work groups and a different approach to traditional assembly-line production. The Volvo company eliminated certain traditional supervisory practices and encouraged direct participation by employees in the day-to-day organization of work. At Woodlawn Mines, near the New South Wales town of Goulburn, a new approach to mining operations was undertaken which involved the development of multi-skilling among employees. The company also introduced the concept of "technical advisors" and "shift co-ordinators" to replace the traditional role of foreman or supervisor. The company's objective was to devise a more effective organization through a "flatter" management structure and the development of a more highly skilled and self-regulated labour force.[15] A modified approach to the use of semi-autonomous work groups is provided by the Siddons Industries case, where the production system was reorganized around a series of cells. Factors that have both promoted and inhibited the development of new forms of work organization, based on the socio-technical systems approach, may be discerned in these three case studies.

Case 6: The Kalmar Assembly Plant

Much has been written about the experience of the Volvo Corporation in Sweden with designing alternative systems for vehicle assembly. This case study deals with the establishment of a new type of assembly plant during the 1970s at Kalmar, a small town on the south-east coast of Sweden. The focus of the study is on the impact the new form of work organization at Kalmar had upon the role of supervisors in the plant. The account of the Kalmar experience given in this study is based upon personal observations made during a visit to the plant in the late 1970s and on various reports published on the project in recent years.

Background to the Kalmar Project

During the late 1960s the Volvo Corporation enjoyed buoyant market conditions which made it possible to expand its production and build new plants. At the same time, however, the company was experiencing a high level of labour turnover, absenteeism, and strike activity at many of its established assembly plants. The unions representing workers in the highly organized Swedish auto industry were also demanding increased influence over decisions affecting the work of their members. During the ealy 1970s, Volvo decided to establish a new assembly plant in a region of Sweden where there was a surplus of people seeking jobs and little existing manufacturing industry. The company also sought to redesign the production system so as to reduce the high level of turnover, absenteeism, and work stoppages which had plagued many of its other assembly plants during the late 1960s and early 1970s.

Discussions were held between the Volvo management and principal unions representing the auto workers before any final decision was made concerning the establishment and design of the new assembly plant. A design team was formed which comprised industrial engineers, supervisors, and union representatives. Attitude surveys were conducted among large numbers of employees at existing plants to obtain their views of requirements at the new plant. The final plans were the product of several years of discussion and negotiations.

Major Features of the New Assembly Plant at Kalmar

When production began in 1974, the Kalmar plant was designed for the assembly of thirty thousand cars a year. There were 636 employees, of whom 540 were directly employed in production. Approximately 10 per cent of the work force was female. The payment system, negotiated between the company and the unions, was based on job evaluation plus a performance component.

One of the main innovations made by Volvo at the new plant was the division of the employees into teams, each of which was responsible for one aspect of the assembly work. There were approximately thirty teams or work groups throughout the plant, each consisting of fifteen to twenty persons. Each team was accountable for a particular function, such as assembly of the electrical system or installing the brakes and wheels, and responsible for deciding how the work should be carried out.

An important technical innovation at the new plant was a battery-powered assembly carrier that functioned both as a transport device and assembly platform. The carriers moved the car bodies through the assembly plant, guided by impulses from a central computer, enabling the teams to exercise considerable flexibility in the organization of their work. The carriers could be halted and guided manually so that assembly could be carried out on stationary vehicles. This was a significant difference from the conventional moving-line and fixed-pace assembly system. The assembly process at Kalmar is shown in more detail in figure 21.

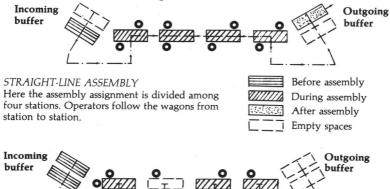

STRAIGHT-LINE ASSEMBLY
Here the assembly assignment is divided among four stations. Operators follow the wagons from station to station.

▤▤▤ Before assembly
▨▨▨ During assembly
▦▦▦ After assembly
⌐ ⌐ Empty spaces

DOCK ASSEMBLY
The entire assembly operation is done at one of the four docks. Two or three workers are in each dock.

Two assembly approaches
The assembly work is organized in two different ways. The most prevalent of the two is *straight-line assembly*, where the work in one team area is divided among four or five stations, placed one after the other in the direction of production flow. The workers operate in groups of two, following a car from station to station and carrying out the entire work assignment belonging to their team. When a two-man group of this kind finishes one car and goes back to the beginning to start on another, the two usually trade places. This means that the work cycle for an assembly worker ranges from 16 to 40 minutes, depending on the number of stations and whether he switches places with his partner.

The other assembly approach is *dock assembly*, meaning that a carrier automatically glides into a dock in an assembly area, where the team's entire assembly assignment is carried out on stationary wagons. Each such assembly dock is manned by two or three persons, who can shift assignments among themselves. The content and the quality of the work done is the same as in straight-line assembly. The only difference is that, in dock assembly, the entire work cycle is done at a single work station, while in straight-line assembly it is divided among several stations.

(Reproduced, by permission, from Aguren, Hansson, and Karlsson, *The Volvo Plant: The Impact of New Design on Work Organisation*, p. 11.)

Figure 21   The assembly process at the Volvo plant in Kalmar, Sweden

The average work cycle at the Kalmar plant was about ten times that of the conventional assembly system and required a greater knowledge of various skills by each assembly worker. The teams were also held responsible for the quality of their work. Closed-circuit television screens, connected to the computer system, fed back information to each team about any defects in their work.

Another feature of the plant was a system of joint consultation between management and employees based on a series of works councils. This type of arrangement exists in all Swedish enterpises with more than fifty employees as a result of collective agreements between the employers and the unions. A works council comprises representatives from management and unions and provides a forum for discussing issues of concern to both parties. There were three major unions represented at Volvo covering the assembly workers, office staff, and supervisors.

The New Role of the Supervisor at Kalmar

One of the most significant differences between conventional assembly lines and the new plant at Kalmar concerned the role of the supervisor. As noted earlier, work teams were the foundation on which the new plant organization was to be developed. The principle of semi-autonomous work groups was, in fact, the starting point for the actual physical design of the plant. Each team was given its own assembly area where it would work and be responsible, within limits, for how it achieved its output. The production targets for the plant were determined by collective bargaining between the unions and the management. Where did this leave the supervisor?

Supervisors and industrial engineers were not included in the teams. They worked in pairs and, for the most part, were responsible for three work teams. The role of the supervisor, however, was less one of control and more one of ensuring that each team had sufficient supplies and information to carry out their work effectively. Within each work team a "team leader" was appointed by management in consultation with the relevant union officials who, in turn, consulted members of each team. The team leaders acted as informal supervisors but also worked as team members. They also acted as spokesmen for their teams and provided a link with other teams. In other words, they were team members with special duties.

It should be noted that the composition and functions of work teams varied within the plant, as did the role of the team leader. Among teams that were responsible for control and adjustment functions, individual tasks were more common. In teams where the work could be carried out simultaneously on both sides of the vehicle, two-person teams were quite common. In straight-line assembly, a two-person team followed each vehicle for four or five stations, and each person carried out half of the total job. Nevertheless, teamwork was still required within the group, co-ordinated by the team leader.

The new forms of work organization were achieved only after long negotiations with the supervisors' union. Initially, the union opposed changes in the supervisor's traditional functions but subsequently switched its strategy to one of seeking an expanded role for the supervisor. One of the major functions fulfilled by the supervisor under the conventional system of vehicle assembly was the negotiation and administration of piece rates. Under the new system, the supervisor was given the broader role of co-ordinating the work of several teams. The transition was not without difficulties but was assisted by the company's willingness to upgrade the status of the supervisor to one of a technical planner and co-ordinator.

An Evaluation of the Kalmar Project

When the new plant opened in 1974, it was estimated to have cost about 10 per cent more than a comparable conventional auto-assembly plant to build. Pehr Gyllenhammer, the president of Volvo, announced that the company's objective was to build a plant that "without any sacrifice of efficiency or financial results, [would] give employees the opportunity to work in groups, to communicate freely, to shift among work assignments, to vary their pace, to identify themselves with the product, to be conscious of responsibility for quality, and to influence their own work environment".[16]

Two years later, Volvo invited the Rationalisation Council, a body comprising representatives from the Swedish central employers' and trade union organizations, to evaluate the results achieved by the new plant. An investigation was conducted over a six-month period, including two months of intensive plant-level research. A major part of the investigation involved interviews with more than a hundred employees at the plant. Although the findings of the council related to the plant as a whole, there were some important implications for the role of the supervisor under the new forms of work organization. The findings of the Rationalisation Council were reported under a number of sub-headings:

Production Efficiency

A comparison between assembly times at the new plant and conventional plants where the same vehicles were assembled revealed no substantial differences. It is important to note, however, that the supervisors and industrial engineers had delegated the job of working out planning details to the teams. According to conventional engineering theory, this should have resulted in longer assembly times, but no differences were found. The main reasons for success at Kalmar in this regard were the reduction of "downtime" and a higher capacity utilization. This was a remarkable achievement in view of the complicated guidance system of assembly carriers. The number of man-hours per car, not immediately influenced by production volume, was somewhat higher at Kalmar compared with conventional plants. However, the control and adjustment work was projected to be less extensive in the future. The corporation also announced its intention to further decentralize this aspect in order to reduce the amount of final adjustment work. Absenteeism among workers at Kalmar during the six months covered by the study was 14 per cent, compared with an average of 19 per cent at other conventional Volvo plants. Labour turnover at the new plant was 16 per cent compared with 21 per cent elsewhere.

The investigators were cautious about drawing conclusions on the basis of these statistics but felt that the results at Kalmar were encouraging. They predicted that efficiency should increase as the plant approached full capacity. Their report therefore endorsed the advantages of a smaller number of supervisors and more flexible production arrangements. They predicted that lower absenteeism and turnover would become even more significant in the future.

Team Organization

The investigators found, almost without exception, that employees reacted favourably to the new method of working in groups. Positive ratings were given by employees to the independence of operation made possible by teamwork, the feeling of unity, and the tolerance shown by team members for each other. However, attitudes did vary towards specific practices within the plant, such as job switching and working ahead for extra breaks.

The practice of job rotation, or job switching, varied between different team areas. In some teams, job rotation was strictly determined by a schedule drawn up by the team members themselves, while in others it occurred spontaneously. A common feature, however, was that most job rotation was motivated by the fact that some jobs were more rigidly spaced, heavier, or more unpleasant than others. Most teams sought to rotate the most arduous jobs to spread them as evenly as possible be'ween group members.

While the rotation of jobs was quite popular, switching teams was not. Although some workers sought to transfer to another team because of differences with other members or the desire to learn new skills, this was relatively uncommon. In order to overcome problems resulting from temporary absenteeism of group members, an "absenteeism pool" was established. The pool also functioned as a form of supervisory training. Workers who wished to learn more skills in order to become a supervisor were encouraged to join the pool. Members of the pool were not tied to a fixed assignment but would be called in as replacements as the need arose.

In order that a planned production level could be maintained by a given work force, the work carried out by each team was calculated to take a fixed amount of time. When less time was used, the operators were regarded as "working ahead". Opportunities to work ahead varied from one team to another. Where components were heavy or tools were fixed at certain work stations, it was more difficult to work ahead. The assembly plant was originally designed to have four buffer places, two before and two after each team. For various technical reasons, however, the buffer system did not work effectively, and some teams interfered with the efforts of other teams to work ahead.

Thus, in general, the individual work teams worked well internally, but there were problems of co-ordination between teams. Individuals were reluctant to switch teams, and some teams interfered with one another's activities. This suggests that supervisors had not been totally successful in co-ordinating the efforts of teams for which they had responsibility.

The Influence of Workers on Job Design and Decision-Making

Although the investigators found that there were more opportunities available to workers to influence the design and organization of work at Kalmar than is usual at conventional assembly plants, their freedom of action was not unlimited. The assembly work was ultimately designed and planned by industrial engineers and co-ordinated by the supervisors. Furthermore, the computer-based control system ensured that the quality of work was closely monitored throughout the assembly process. Agreement on production levels was reached at higher levels between the company and the unions. Frustration with the system manifested itself from time to time. On one occasion there was an unofficial strike by the assembly workers over what they regarded as a reduction in their wages when they failed to reach their production target. At another time, workers protested against the impersonal methods by which the computer provided them with feedback on their performance.

The investigators reported that approximately one-third of workers interviewed felt that they had considerable opportunities to influence their work situation, one-third claimed that they had some opportunities, and one-third felt that their opportunities were inadequate. More than two-thirds of respondents maintained that they would like to have greater opportunities for direct influence. Several reasons were advanced by workers for their failure to exercise greater influence in the workplace. Firstly, since the assembly methods at Kalmar were already highly developed, it was difficult to change them. Secondly, some workers felt that the industrial engineers were unwilling to alter the design of the system in order to accommodate their demands. Thirdly, there were complaints that the works councils functioned mainly as an information forum rather than as a channel for decision-making. Finally, worker representatives often failed to inform their co-workers about the council's deliberations.

Thus, it would appear that although workers had a greater opportunity to influence their work situation at Kalmar, decision-making still remained firmly in the hands of management. Furthermore, although the supervisor was less powerful in the new plant, the industrial engineer retained a significant influence over job design and plant operations.

Implications of the Kalmar Project for the Role of the Supervisor

This case study of the new assembly process at Kalmar has highlighted the central role played by supervisors when introducing new forms of work organization. Although greater formal responsibility was given to work groups or teams for the organization and execution of their tasks, supervision remained a focal issue.

At Kalmar, the number of "formal" supervisors was reduced and aspects of their traditional or conventional role were transferred to the work teams. Within each team, however, team leaders functioned as informal supervisors. An important feature of the new plant was that the team leader was appointed by the management in consultation with the relevant union. In theory, therefore, the teams were able to have strong influence over both their supervision and leadership. The Rationalisation Council, which evaluated the effects of changes in the new plant, reported that one-third of the workers who were interviewed were dissatisfied with the amount of opportunities to influence their work situation, while two-thirds wanted more direct involvement in decision-making.

Although Volvo sought to upgrade the status and broaden the responsibilities of supervisors, there appeared to be difficulties among supervisors adjusting to their new role. According to one observer, the new supervisor operated "more like a works foreman . . . reporting directly to the plant engineer". In reality, however, major parts of the supervisor's new role appeared to be carried out either by the team leaders or the industrial engineers. Another problem area with the new assembly system appeared to be the co-ordination of activities between the groups, especially in relation to using the buffers. This was a specific part of the "new" role which should have been carried out by the supervisor.

Volvo appear to have used the absenteeism pool as a major source of recruitment and training for supervisors at Kalmar. Since most workers appeared to prefer to stay with their team and resented switching or rotating between teams, the pool did not appear to be an efficient means of building up a resource of future supervisors. Thus, although the new Kalmar plant has been successful in many respects, effective supervision remains a major problem. One unintended consequence of reducing the importance of the formal supervision function has been to increase the informal power of the team leader. The most significant source of control, however, appears to rest with the industrial engineers. The success of the Kalmar plant will depend largely on how the relationships between the supervisors, the industrial engineers, and the team leaders are resolved. It may be some time yet before their respective roles in the new form of work organization at Kalmar become clearly defined.

Case 7: Woodlawn Mines*

In 1967 two subsidiaries of American mining companies began mineral exploration in Australia. This exploration resulted in

---

* Some names and certain data in this case have been disguised to protect the anonymity of the respondents.

samples taken from an area of grazing country near Goulburn, New South Wales, showing economically significant amounts of copper, lead, zinc, and silver. The exploration company formed by the two American parents began test drilling in November 1969. After extensive test drilling over a period of several years, the decision was made to develop and mine the area. Another large Australian-controlled mining company accepted an invitation to participate in the project, and a joint venture agreement between these three companies came into effect on 1 January 1976. Final design was completed, and plant construction began in 1976. Plant commissioning was completed in 1978; full production was achieved in 1979.

During three shifts a day, five days a week, the ore is mined from an open cut planned to reach 600 metres in diameter and 200 metres in depth. A total of eight giant mine haul trucks, each carrying up to 77 tonnes of ore, are loaded in the open cut and travel up the benches cut into the side of the mine to a crusher into which the ore is tipped directly from the trucks. Here the ore is crushed into "intermediate screenings" with a maximum size of 13 millimetres. The crushing plant handles two distinct ores, one a copper-bearing ore and the other a complex ore bearing copper, lead, and zinc. The capacity of the crushing plant is 420 tonnes an hour, and it operates for ten shifts each week. From the crusher the ore is moved by pipeline to the fine-ore storage bins and then onto the mill for processing. In the mill the two types of ore are again processed separately. The copper ore is ground with water in a drum-shaped mill filled with small hardened steel balls. This process separates the copper-bearing mineral which is then separated from the waste by a flotation process. The complex ore is also ground with water in a rod mill and then in the ball mill, which separates the zinc-bearing mineral, the lead-bearing mineral, and the copper-bearing mineral from each other and from the waste material. Again the valuable minerals are retrieved by flotation — copper first, then lead, then zinc. This flotation process is rather complicated and requires about twelve different flotation reagents. The water content of the four concentrates produced is then reduced from about 80 per cent to 8 per cent by using thickeners, filters, and rotary driers. These operations in the mill continue twenty-four hours a day seven days a week. From the mill the dried concentrate is moved by truck to a railhead ten kilometres from the mine. Some of the concentrate is refined at Port Kembla and Whyalla and some is exported.

Annual production at Woodlawn is about 1 million tonnes of combined complex ore (producing zinc concentrate, lead concentrate, and two grades of copper concentrate) and approximately 7 million tonnes of waste. The metal contained in this output is 70,000 tonnes of zinc, 20,000 tonnes of lead, 12,000 tonnes of copper, and 26,000 kilograms of silver. Proved ore reserves in 1979 were established at 10 million tonnes of sulphides. The total costs to establish the mine was $78 million.

Management Philosophy at Woodlawn Mines

The original general manager at Woodlawn Mines believed that people are motivated not only by money but also by other factors such as the nature of the work itself, the possibility for personal growth, and the opportunity for achievement, advancement, and recognition. When setting up the organization structure at Woodlawn, the general manager planned to implement this broad philosophy by adopting two main goals:

1. To set up a corporate structure so that responsibility for many operating decisions remained at a relatively low level within the organization
2. To provide opportunities for operator growth and achievement by multi-skilling and paying for those skills.

Woodlawn was in an ideal position to be innovative because in 1978 and 1979 there was local unemployment, so most of the work force comprised young rural men and women who were inexperienced in the traditional mining working environment.

During the plant commissioning stage in 1978, the employee relations group became aware of some Australian research done into the relative importance of various work values. A relatively small group of Woodlawn operators were then asked to rank

these work values and quite similar results were obtained. Most important job values were:
- Work that gives you a feeling of having done a job well
- Work in which you can create something new
- Work in which you can learn more about how things work

This research confirmed the feelings of the top management at the mine that a non-traditional method of management and supervision should be tried at Woodlawn. The first step was to establish a much flatter line organization. Under the general manager are six major functional areas: the mine, the mill, engineering, administration, geology, and employee relations. Figure 22 takes engineering as an example and contrasts the

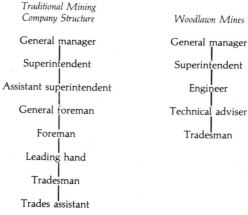

Figure 22 Organizational structure of engineering operations at Woodlawn Mines compared with a traditional mining company

number of levels within the engineering function at Woodlawn with the number in the traditional mining engineering operation; three levels of direct supervision in the traditional structure (the general foreman, the foreman, and the leading hand) are compressed into one level at Woodlawn (the technical adviser). Gus Johnson, the personnel and training co-ordinator at Woodlawn, described how it developed:

"In our small survey, these farmers — girls from Goulburn, and other locals — said that doing a job well was number one and that work in which they can learn something new and create something was next. So we decided to go ahead, and we had to decide how to change the organization. We eliminated the general foreman and the foreman, and from these two positions we have created a fellow called a technical adviser or shift co-ordinator. This is certainly unheard of in the mining industry.

"We have also done something else. If we eliminate leading hands — and remember, we want to push decision-making to the lowest possible level — we create the problem that the people at this level, the operators and the tradesmen, will not be well enough informed to be able to make decisions about their work. So we had to train them.

"But we also had other reasons for training our operators. Changing technology was forcing us to train them. For example, the fellow who is working the back wheel of a Wabco truck in the Pilbara region of Western Australia becomes a very specialized tradesman — so specialized that we consider him as becoming de-skilled, particularly if that truck doesn't exist next year. So in a way 'experienced' people don't exist, because they are becoming de-skilled. They certainly don't exist in the Goulburn area, and that's really another reason for training. There was a local unemployment problem, and we wanted to be good Goulburn neighbours and do something about that.[17] So we decided to take the various constraints that were on us and use them to our advantage."

The Training Programme at Woodlawn

Every task in the four main operating areas of the mine (the open cut, the mill, the engineering workshop, and the warehouse) was carefully defined and then groups of related tasks were combined into what became known as operating areas. When these operating areas were first set up in 1978, there were ten in the mine, twelve in the mill, three in engineering, and six in the warehouse. During 1979 the operating areas were revised to those shown in table 11.

In addition to this task analysis, the company carried out a

Table 11 Operating areas at Woodlawn

MINE	MILL	ENGINEERING	WAREHOUSE
1. Auxiliary services	1. Crushing	1. Electrical	1. Basic warehouse functions
2. Equipment services	2. Grinding	2. Instrumentation	2. Developed warehouse functions
3. Haul road services	3. Floation — copper lead	3. Mobile equipment	3. Advanced warehouse functions
4. Primary dozing	4. Floation — copper zinc	4. Fixed plant	4. Cataloguing
5. Primary drilling	5. Dewatering	5. Component rebuild	5. EDP
6. Primary hauling	6. Reagents		6. Inventory central
7. Primary loading	7. Concentrate load out		7. Procurement
8. Explosives/ survey/ sampling	8. Mobile equipment		8. Warehouse management
	9. Services		
	10. Operations repairs		
	11. Central control room operations		
	12. Analytical laboratory		
	13. Metallurgical laboratory		
	14. Pilot plant		
	15. Utility		
	16. Sampling		

training needs analysis which Gus Johnson described as a "well recognized, systematic approach to training where we established operational needs and then clearly specified objectives and finally determined what type of training was needed to achieve those objectives". The operational needs were established from the task analysis, and the specific training was developed in terms of units with detailed behavioural objectives. These training units provide operators with a range of skills; hence the term *multi-skilling*. A mine operator, for example, becomes multi-skilled horizontally in the sense that he learns to operate a variety of equipment — haulage trucks, dozers, and loaders — and also multi-skilled vertically as he learns more about each separate skill — mechanics of machines, machine repair as well as operation, pit geology, and surveying.

Permanent training staff from the company's Employee Relations Department as well as supervisors (shift co-ordinators, technical advisers) and sometimes skilled operators themselves conduct the company's formalized training sessions. These sessions are held in classrooms and on the job and also often take the form of self-directed study. Evaluation of these training sessions is done by the instructor or by the supervisor on the job. This evaluation process also provides input to a periodic re-evaluation of the needs analysis. The cyclical process which results from this process is shown in figure 23.

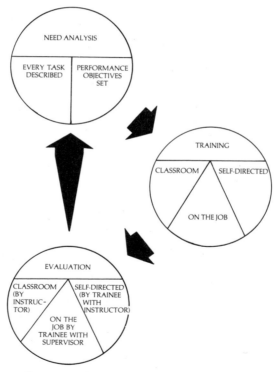

Figure 23   The training programme at Woodlawn

Industrial Relations at Woodlawn

Multi-skilling did present a potential problem with the unions. A typical mine might have as many as seventy-two job classifications with a range of unions, each rather particular about the domain of the jobs performed by its members. So at Woodlawn the potential for demarcation problems was great. In order to avoid these problems, an industrial agreement was worked out between Woodlawn Mines and the three unions on the site — the Australian Workers' Union (AWU), the Amalgamated Metal, Foundry and Shipwrights' Union (AMFSU), and the Electrical Trades Union of Australia (ETU). This agreement contained a clause that had not appeared in any previous similar agreement in the mining industry in Australia. Clause 4 contained only five job classifications — general hand, mine, mill, warehouse, and engineering — and within the four classifications mine, mill, warehouse, and engineering were detailed five levels of training. An untrained operator enters one of these areas at level 5 and progresses through to level 1 after a period of four years of highly structured training. In the words of Gus Johnson: "We have a payment for skill rather than a payment for service or a payment for classification. We have a very simple classification system — you are employed as a general hand, plant tradesman, electrician, operator, or warehouseman. That gives us tremendous flexibility. We have no trades assistants; no speciality trades. We have one agreement with all our unions."

The way the whole system was established is shown in figure 24. This system should achieve the twin objectives of setting responsibility at a relatively low level in the organization and of providing opportunities for operator growth and achievement by multi-skilling. Clause 4 of the agreement makes the detailed implementation of the programme clear to all concerned with it.

Implementation of Multi-skilling at Woodlawn

Jim **Padgett** is the day shift co-ordinator at the mill. He has to co-ordinate the work of thirteen of the thirty-eight operators

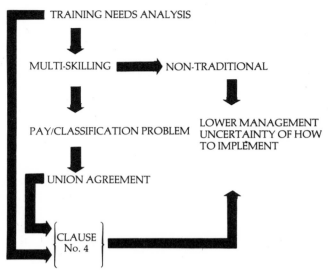

Figure 24   The management system at Woodlawn

employed in the mill. "Candor is the biggest difference between Woodlawn and BHP [Padgett's previous position was with BHP] — the ability to cross-communicate. You can approach anyone. But to get my operators to be the same with me is still a big problem." Jim Padgett believes that almost all of the operators at the mill are there for the money and not for a career. "If no one turns up to replace an operator at the end of a shift, he or she will not stay on as I will. We cannot make operators accountable because of the award. As soon as something goes wrong, the situation requires hands-on supervision." In fact, while Padgett believes that "multi-skilling will work in time" he feels that "it would be better to have mining people, as the current operators are not production oriented".

The senior metallurgist, Alf Robertson, has even stronger views about the new system: "The system of autonomous work groups hasn't worked. In fact, in the mill here we've had to go back to the more traditional shift boss system."

This reaction contrasts with the experience of Bob Watson,

acting technical adviser in the workshop (part of the engineering department). When asked if the new system provided a different work environment for his men, he replied: "They don't work for me; we all work together. But there is much greater job satisfaction for the co-ordinator and for the sparkies [electricians]. You don't have two or three people on your back all the time — if you do the job, that's all there is to it".

Gus Johnson thinks the nature of the work itself may have something to do with these rather different reactions: "In the mine, turnover is only 3 or 4 per cent. In engineering it's almost nil. In metallurgy [the mill], however, it's almost 30 per cent. We thought it might be the shift work, because there were a lot of complaints from people not familiar with shift work — they can't get to football practice, for example. But we also work shifts in the mine, so perhaps it's the nature of the work. I think it's probably a more comfortable job to sit in a machine which has a cabin and moves around rather than to be working in fairly dirty conditions in the mill."

Selection and training of co-ordinators is another area where some uncertainty still exists. As Johnson explained, all co-ordinators "are recruited, in addition to their technical competence, on the understanding that they have some motive for trying to link management and the workers in a better way than has been done traditionally". But initial estimates of the number of operators required were too low, and as a result there have been too few co-ordinators on the site.

Operations pressures on the co-ordinators have been great. In addition, their training created some pressures as it comprised "being thrown into the concepts of the managerial grid (see chap. 5). The exact role of the co-ordinator has never been explicitly stated. "We've allowed it to evolve, and that process of evolution has been a bit painful." Gus Johnson believes "the co-ordinator will become an internal consultant, in terms of both role and style, effective enough to have his semi-autonomous work group functioning to the point where he is no longer required."

The co-ordinator plays an important part in the training programme. As well as conducting some of the in-class training sessions himself, he has also had to conduct and evaluate on-the-job and semi-directed training. One co-ordinator in the mine every so often has a Saturday morning meeting in Goulburn, when his whole group discusses training and development.

Gus Johnson explains the operation of the training programmes as follows: "We teach the tradesman to operate the machine as well as teaching the operator to do some basic maintenance. Traditionally, the operator would drive the machine right into the workshop bay, where the mechanic would fix it. Now the operator will get a fitter on the radio, and the fitter will come up to the mine and get the machine. He then takes the operator with him, and the operator tends to work as his trades assistant. We are always encouraging them to help each other and to learn from one another.

"We put every operator who shows an interest through the 'methods of instruction' training. They can learn to write objectives for courses and teach the courses. Some of them have a flair for it in the classroom, and some don't. Teaching on the job varies much more — sometimes it goes very well and other times it's bloody awful. We don't yet monitor it well enough, but we are working on how to do it better."

Although the new system of work organization at Woodlawn Mines is still evolving, the concept of multi-skilling is now well entrenched. The attitudes of the elected shop stewards to clause 4 (which covers multi-skilling) during the renegotiation of the Woodlawn industrial agreement are reported by Gus Johnson in these terms: "They questioned clause 4, but only in the sense they wanted to refine it. They could see ways to improve it based on their experience. So the ten operating areas in the mine became eight, and the twelve operating areas in the mill became sixteen. We were somewhat afraid they might question the hell out of it and force us back to a traditional system, but they didn't. They saw that with this new system they had wide learning opportunities, and they accepted it." Woodlawn Mines offers an interesting alternative to traditional forms of management. It remains to be seen whether it becomes a model for others to follow.

Case 8: Siddons Industries

Siddons Industries Ltd has progressively introduced principles of industrial democracy, beginning in 1958 with a works council at its Sidchrome plant. Industrial democracy is viewed by John Siddons, chairman of Siddons Industries, in two ways: to increase productivity and to improve the quality of the workplace. He emphasized that "the humanization of the workplace and productivity should not be seen to be contradictory."

During 1975 John Siddons developed a six-point plan of industrial democracy with the aim of achieving these twin goals of humanization and productivity. The six areas were:
1. Worker representation on the board of directors
2. Profit sharing
3. Employee share purchase
4. Establishment of a works council
5. Flexible working hours
6. Shop-floor democracy using a cellular organization structure

Some progress has been made in all these areas. The works council consists of fourteen members — nine elected by the employees and five nominated by management. A successful experiment on flexible working hours, which involves employees working a $9\frac{1}{3}$-hour day for four days each, was introduced in 1979. It had not been implemented on a permanent basis at the time of writing, however, owing to the overtime bans that had been imposed as part of the union's 35-hour week campaign. In 1981, 10 per cent of Siddons shares were owned by the employees. The target for employee share ownership is 15 per cent. Profit sharing and the cellular organization structure are interrelated and have a significant impact on the first-line manager. Substantial changes have occurred at the Siddons Heidelberg plant in these areas since 1975.

Cellular Organization

Work groups or cells were established at Sidchrome on the premise that workers will be more satisfied and productive if they are permitted, within limits, to manage their own work activities. The company established groups of about forty people with clearly stated responsibilities for hiring, assigning work, allocating overtime, planning work loads, purchasing parts and raw materials, and setting production goals. Within each cell at Sidchrome there are three distinct levels of employee: the cell leader or product manager; the technical specialists, such as engineers, draughtsmen, toolmakers, and foremen; and the process workers.

Before 1975, the Heidelberg factory was organized along fairly traditional lines, with a works manager having line control of all plant operations. With the introduction of the cellular structure in 1975, the works manager's position was eliminated and replaced by a series of product managers (product manager — sockets, product manager — rings, product manager — ring open-ended, and product manager — accessories), together with the laboratory manager, the maintenance engineer, and the services manager. This structure is shown in figure 25. These cell leaders reported to the assistant general manager, whose primary task was co-ordination and ensuring that the competition between cells did not become "destructive". With the increased competition from imports and the resulting decline in demand during the latter half of the 1970s came a reduction in the size of the four manufacturing cells. In 1980 a decision was made to amalgamate the rings and ring open-ended cells and the sockets and accessories cells. This reduction to two manufacturing cells resulted in a more effective utilization of the technical resources attached to each cell.

John Siddons described the eventual aim of the cellular structure as being the establishment of "profit centres related to small groups of people". He concluded: "I am convinced that a cellular structure will work better if it embraces the entire organization, not just the shop floor, and I am convinced that the only way that can be done is financially through profit centres. Each cell or group works on a product line and then through a mechanism of transfer prices 'sells' the product to the next group. These transfer prices relate to the true profitability of the plant." As of mid-1981 the company had a bonus scheme

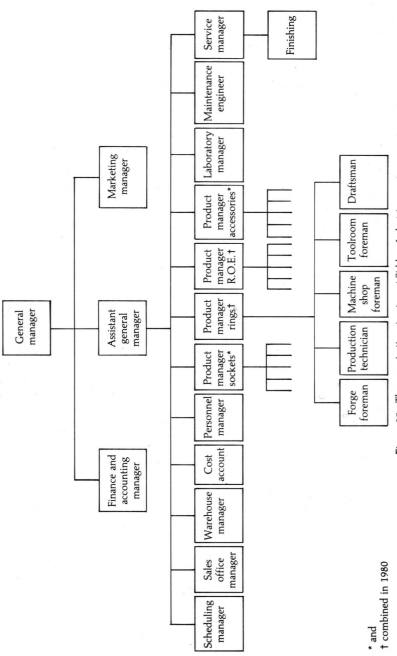

Figure 25 The organization structure at Siddons Industries

* and
† combined in 1980

for management down to, but not including, the foreman level. Profit-sharing is to be introduced for the process workers within each cell; the payment received by each worker will be directly related to the profitability of the particular cell.

Making a hand tool involves four basic stages. First the design for the product is developed. Next the machine tools required to make the product can be scheduled which involves two basic steps: the forging of the basic product shape, and the machining of the final product. The product then goes into bulk storage and is packed and shipped against customer orders. For each major product group all the four basic manufacturing processes are the responsibility of the product manager (see fig. 26). As John Siddons explained: "We try to have all the exper-

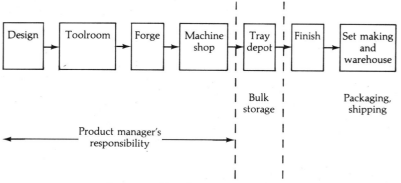

Figure 26   Manufacturing process flow

tise to make a particular product within the one cell. So they do not have to call to any great extent on outside areas for services. For example, in the socket area the forging equipment, the machines to make dies, and the machinery to machine the forgings are all there, and the cell in effect subcontracts the heat treatment."

Experience with the cellular structure has generated a number of benefits over a more traditional structure. Robert Hawkes, one of the manufacturing product managers, sees the two major benefits as being the ability to focus his attention in a smaller area ("I don't have to worry about the socket area") and better co-ordination of the material flow on the shop floor ("Now I have a couple of draftsmen in my cell who do our own design work — so I can very quickly solve any problems which might arise between design and the toolroom"). A more general benefit is that "the survival of the cell is very much everyone's business". Robert Hawkes explained: "There is none of the attitude that 'those blokes over there don't know what they are doing, but we have no control over them and so we just have to lump it'. For example, everyone takes some part in product development, tooling development. It is *not* the province of one individual. The toolroom foreman co-ordinates between drafting, his own toolroom, and production."

John Siddons believes the cell structure has increased the degree of innovation: "They have the responsibility within the cell to do whatever will improve productivity. The cell leader leaves to the group members as many of the decisions as possible. And that is why they are innovative. They are closer to the job, and they can generally see the most cost-effective thing to do." But there are also some disadvantages. There has been a certain amount of infighting between the groups, particularly over shared resources such as the final heat treatment (performed by the service manager's cell). Competition between cells for capital investment in machinery and equipment has also been fierce, although this competition has diminished since the reduction in the number of cells.

When the cells were established, the product managers were selected by the Sidchrome management with the aim of "obtaining the best leaders". One of the new product managers came from the shop floor. Robert Hawkes sees his main role as a product manager "as a co-ordinator between the forge foreman, the production technician, the machine shop foreman, and drafting". His other major areas of concern are liaison with marketing on meeting order due dates, quality control and assurance, and new product development. Co-ordination between cells is achieved through a weekly meeting of the two manufacturing cell product managers, the services manager, the assistant general manager, and occasionally the general manager.

The role of the foreman has changed with the introduction of the cellular structure. As Robert Hawkes explained: "We still have a traditional foreman, leading hand, employee structure — there is nothing unique about that. But the role of the foreman has changed quite a lot with the introduction of the cellular structure. There is now far more awareness of the problems of one foreman by the other foremen. For example, the foreman of the machine shop has a much better understanding of the problems of the forge foreman because they have to work together as a team to get the product out in the most efficient manner." For the rings/ring open-ended cell, the machine shop foreman does the detailed daily production scheduling.[18] Robert Hawkes commented: "He is in the best position to know exactly how we are doing and to schedule accordingly."

Results

After the first twelve months of operating with the cellular structure, productivity had increased by 15 per cent, workers' compensation cases had decreased by 26 per cent, labour turnover was down by 46 per cent, and absenteeism had fallen by 13 per cent. From 1975 to 1980 the number of employees at the Heidelberg factory had been reduced from around eight hundred to four hundred. Almost all of this decrease had been absorbed by natural wastage. But despite this reduction in the work force, the output level in 1980 was only marginally below the all-time peak level of 1972.

PART 3

CONCLUSIONS

8

Prospects for the First-Line Manager and Organizational Change

As noted earlier in this book, the "problem of the supervisor" has been the subject of considerable research and discussion for many years. In a recent British study, Child and Partridge argued that "over the past hundred years . . . the once clearly recognizable occupational role enjoyed by the foreman as workshop manager has become transformed into the confusion of role conflicts, of specialist encroachments, and disparities between managerial theory and practice, which so often surround his contemporary equivalent, the supervisor".[1] Based upon the work of Child and Partridge, four possible approaches to the future development of the supervisory role are outlined below. While the four approaches are by no means exhaustive, they provide useful approximations to expected future practice. Whichever approach emerges as the dominant one in the future will depend upon the prevailing circumstances.

The Changing Supervisory Role: Possible Alternatives

1. The supervisor as a first-line manager. This approach finds its strongest expression in the German concept of the *Meister*, who generally has a higher level of qualifications and greater degree of authority than the Anglo-American or Australian supervisor. The *Meister* will usually have served a skilled apprenticeship, followed by several years as a skilled worker, and will have obtained a formal qualification in foremanship by examination. The status of a *Meister* in Germany, both as a skilled worker and first-line manager, is protected by law. According to Maurice, Sorge, and Warner,[2] differences in supervisory roles between Germany and other countries reflect cultural differences in systems of education, training, recruitment, and promotion. Furthermore, the *Meister* is generally given responsibility and authority over matters that would be the prerogative of staff specialists and higher-level managers in many other countries.

Upgrading the supervisor to the level of first-line manager, in the Australian context, would mean not only enlarging the scope of the position but also shedding some minor aspects of the existing supervisory role. It is possible that a number of functions currently carried out by supervisors, such as the provision of materials and equipment, record-keeping, and so on, could be delegated to work groups. On the other hand, it is possible that the leading hand or assistant supervisor would simply inherit the left-over aspects of the supervisor's job. The latter development would not only create dissatisfaction among the leading hands but also could result in further levels of supervision being created.

As the work force has become more educated and changes in technology have required more sophisticated forms of organization, the trend towards a more "managerial" role for the supervisor has increased. There are limits, nevertheless, on the extent to which major decisions can be delegated to the level of the first-line manager. Production systems that are highly complex and interdependent, for example, may be difficult to manage effectively at the section or department level. The degree to which supervisors develop a managerial role at the workplace level will therefore be determined by a variety of organizational and external factors.

2. The supervisor as a sub-manager. Numerous commentators have drawn attention to the irony that, while the formal status of many supervisors has been raised to the level of "first-line manager", their actual authority and responsibilities have been progressively diminished. Hence, supervisors are increasingly held accountable as managers while being excluded from many managerial decisions. Child and Partridge note that "supervisors today experience something of a double standard when they compare how the ideology expresses their relationship to management with the way this actually operates . . . Management has formally removed responsibilities from supervisors to specialists without necessarily recognizing that those supervisors still have to deal with the application of specialist activities to the shop floor or office under their charge."[3] It is argued, therefore, that there should be a clearer definition of the supervisory role and the restoration of authority to the position. This does not mean that supervisors should be raised to the level of "management" but that their role should be recognized as a specialist "sub-managerial" one.

Jaques[4] advocates that the supervisor should assist the manager in training, recruiting, and assessing subordinates, in scheduling work, allocating employees to jobs, and setting out appropriate methods. Although supervisors may recommend actions to managers, and oversee the work of subordinates, they do not have the authority to make policy. This approach is bureaucratic and relies upon formal organizational rules. Its attraction lies in the fact that it provides the supervisor with an important sub-managerial role. The difficulty of applying such a literal and rigid approach within organizations, however, is that it is rarely easy to make such clear distinctions between supervisory and managerial roles. This is particularly the case in a dynamic environment where work roles change rapidly and cannot be rigidly defined.

3. The supervisor as a technical specialist or professional. This approach attempts to redefine the supervisory role to increase its relevance in a rapidly changing environment. There are two main variants of this model. One is when the supervisor has particular technical or craft skills that are relevant to the work situation. In some cases, the supervisor may have skills or experience that are not available to senior management. A typical example of this situation is where a skilled tradesman supervises the work of maintenance workers and reports to a manager who is qualified in a different field of expertise. The supervisor, in this context, has the potential to achieve considerable status as a technical expert in the eyes of both the people whose work he or she supervises and the manager to whom he or she reports.

The second variant is where the supervisor co-ordinates the work of a diverse team whose fields of expertise are complementary. In this situation the supervisor acts in the role of an "integrator", whose success relies not only on his or her level of technical expertise but also on his or her ability to create an effective team. A typical example would be a research and development group composed of people with a wide range of experience and qualifications who are brought together to work on a particular problem. In this case the supervisor may also be an active member of the team, contributing ideas to the project, as well as taking responsibility for the overall output of the group. The "supervisor as expert" is likely to be found most commonly where the tasks are reasonably complex and where the supervisor is required to operate in a relatively independent or autonomous fashion.

4. The supervisor as a work group co-ordinator or adviser. This approach gained momentum in the 1970s with the introduction of semi-autonomous work groups, particularly in Scandinavian countries. The theory underlying this approach was that work groups would be given the freedom to appoint their own leaders, allocate work between members of the group, and undertake their own quality control and maintenance tasks. The elected work group leaders, who might be former supervisors, would act as advisers to work groups on technical matters, procedures, training, and so on. However, they would respond to the demands of the work group rather than acting on behalf of management. The benefits sought by this change included the improvement of communications through the abolition of one managerial level, providing openings for untapped potential from the shop floor, enhancing participation in decision-making, and improving the quality of work life.

The results of experiments in abolishing the supervisory role have been varied. In Norway, problems arose with the introduction of semi-autonomous work groups, without participation by supervisors, when internal conflicts over matters such as work allocation were not resolved. Even where supervisors were transformed into team or work-group advisers, pro-

blems arose over the extent to which the supervisor should in-
tervene. In Sweden, where supervisors have tended to retain a
stronger role in semi-autonomous work groups, the problems
have been less severe. Nevertheless, there are situations where
a scaling down of the traditional supervisory role and the corresponding development of greater work-group autonomy
appears to be effective. Two of the case studies presented in
this book, Woodlawn Mines and the Kalmar plant, provide ex-
cellent examples of semi-autonomous work groups in action. In
each case, however, significant effort has been devoted to
upgrading the skills of employees to enable them to undertake
many of the roles formerly performed by the traditional
supervisors.

   It is clear from the research evidence presented in this book
that there are essentially two broad types of first-line managers
at work in Australian industry and commerce, which cut across
the four categories presented by Child and Partridge. The
primary differentiating variable is career orientation. One
group of first-line managers are younger and aspiring to future
careers in the upper levels of management. The other group are
older, having spent most of their working life on the factory
floor, and consider their supervisory position as the apex of
their careers. An interesting aspect of the research was that the
"managerially" oriented supervisors were generally younger
and held more senior positions in larger organizations. They
were also better educated and favoured a more participative,
employee-centred supervisory style. The "supervisory"
oriented first-line managers favoured a more traditional
authoritarian style of supervision, were older, less formally
educated, worked in smaller organizations, and supervised
more people.

   The first-line manager performs his or her function within a
complex network of structures and interactions. A basic conclusion drawn from the research reported in this book is that the
first-line manager's role is situationally dependent. Bob Watson,
the technical adviser in the workshop at Woodlawn Mines, for
example, may not have operated as successfully at Mount
Newman Mines as he did at Woodlawn. Different environ-

ments tend to foster or support particular management styles. This final chapter will examine the organizational context and structure within which first-line managers operate and relate it to their supervisory styles and roles. This examination and the resulting paradigm relies heavily on the survey research and the case study analyses presented in the earlier parts of this book.

An important conclusion drawn from our research is that the most appropriate behaviour and role of the first-line managers are related to the basic objectives and strategy of the employing organization. While the series of links joining organizational strategy and supervisory role often may not be clearly specified, the relationship is nevertheless important. In essence, the linkage occurs in a number of steps: the most appropriate supervisory role is dependent upon the type or physical characteristics of the manufacturing or processing system; the dominant type of manufacturing or processing system is dependent upon overall corporate strategy; and overall corporate strategy, in turn, is dependent upon environmental conditions and the availability of resources.

Systems of Production and Managerial Roles

Using Joan Woodward's original categorization of production types,[5] William Westley has argued that the role of the supervisor is related to the nature of the production system.[6] The skills and abilities required of the supervisor differ according to whether he or she is supervising a unit production, a batch production, or a continuous process production operation. In an operation that produces individual items or small batches to order, the supervisor should act primarily as a technical adviser. Large batch production involves specialized and narrowly defined tasks performed by a relatively unskilled work force. This environment requires a supervisor who will act as a disciplinarian ensuring that the work is completed on time and according to specification. A continuous process production system requires the workers to act as machine tenders and the supervisor as a co-ordinator. Details of this schema are shown in table 12. Westley further argues that with recent technological

Table 12   The impact of production systems on aspects of work organization

Aspects of Work Organization	Unit Production	Large Batch Production Systems	Continuous Process Production
Assigning tasks to workers	Worker completes whole job	Workers highly specialized to narrow tasks — based on industrial engineering	Work is done by automated machines, workers tend the machine
What is needed from labour	Skills and energy	Energy and obedience	Knowledge and responsibility
Effective control system	Foreman is a leader, sets pace and quality, acts as technical adviser	Foreman is supervisor, disciplinarian, sees that workers do as told and work hard	Foreman acts as co-ordinator and adviser; such workers are semi-autonomous, self-managing
Examples	Custom machine shop	Mass production assembly plants production lines	Automated paint line or assembly line, petro-chemical plant

Source: W.A. Westley, *The Role of the Supervisor* (Ottawa: Ministry of Labour, 1981), p. 5.

change, much of the manufacturing sector is acquiring characteristics of the continuous process production system. As a consequence, the role of the supervisor will need to change towards that of a co-ordinator. In Australia, however, relatively few continuous process production plants exist. Most of Australian manufacturing is done in small plants using small or large batch production methods. This fact, together with the research results, emphasizes the importance of understanding that the supervisory role is situationally dependent. There is no one "best" supervisory style or role. In order to explore this idea further in the Australian context, it is necessary to define the predominant types of production systems that exist in Australia and influence the development of supervisory roles.

As previously indicated, our study clearly identified two major types of first-line managers which were labelled "supervisory" and "managerial". In general terms, the "supervisory" type of manager tended to have been promoted from the shop floor and to be at the apex of his or her career. This type of first-line manager tended to regard the immediate task as more important than the human relationships involved and saw his or her primary role as getting the work out on time at an acceptable level of quality. The "managerial" supervisor, on the other hand, was generally younger and more highly educated and had expectations of upward career mobility. This type of supervisor typically showed greater concern for human relationships, while not ignoring the importance of task-related objectives.

The types of production or manufacturing systems most commonly found in Australia can be classified into four categories: continuous flow, assembly line, job shop, and project. Continuous flow describes operations that are virtually continuous and usually highly automated. Oil refineries, float glass making, paper making, and steel production are examples of this type of process. Assembly and fabrication lines involve very large volumes associated with highly specialized short-cycle job tasks. The production of canned soups, domestic appliances, biscuits, or motor cars typically involves an assembly line. The majority of Australian manufacturing establishments, however, are job shops. A job shop is typically set out according to machine types — lathes in one area, grinders in another, drills in another. The volume of any particular product is usually not large, and each of the wide variety of products requires a different path through the plant's complement of machines. Pumps, hand tools and timber windows and doors, for example, are made in a job shop. The final category of production operation is the project system of manufacturing. A single "product" is usually made, one at a time. Each is typically large and complex and requires a sizeable commitment of resources over a reasonable time period. Commercial buildings (offices, retail shopping centres, industrial facilities) and large, one-off products such as aeroplanes, boilers, and some military equipment are produced using a project manufacturing system.

Organizational Characteristics and First-Line Management

Characteristics of the work organization created by these types of manufacturing processes tend to favour one of the two managerial orientations identified in the present study. From our research, and with support from a number of overseas research studies,[7] the dominant characteristics that have been identified as affecting supervisory styles are task structure, the control system, and authority allocation.

With continuous flow production, the task structure required is not very complex because the production process itself is automated and the job involves monitoring a range of operating characteristics. Assembly line production is set up on the basis of a small and highly repetitive work cycle in which the task structure is simple. A job shop normally involves a slightly more complex task structure than the assembly line. Jobs arrive at machine centres in reasonably large batches; each operator performs a relatively limited range of tasks on a single machine. Group technology, which has been described in chapter 6, significantly alters this typical structure and makes the task structure more complex. In a project type of manufacturing system the task structure is complex and a large amount of task repetition is not possible because of the small volume of production.

The extent and nature of the formal control procedures associated with a particular area of work directly affect the degree of autonomy which both the workers and their supervisors are able to exercise on the job. The control procedures are likely to be determined by the size of the organization, the geographical dispersion of the organization's facilities, and its overall corporate goals and objectives, rather than by the nature of the manufacturing process. For example, a company with several manufacturing facilities spread throughout Australia is more likely to have a highly structured and detailed control system than is a single plant operation. Furthermore, a company that faces strong price competition is more likely to have a highly structured control system than a company that has a product tailored specifically to highly variable customer requirements.

Finally, the allocation of authority within the organization is important. If the effective authority or locus of effective decision-making is removed from the workplace, the autonomy of both the workers and supervisors is reduced. This factor, like control systems, is dependent upon strategic issues. A company competing on the basis of the price of its products does not want authority for product design, scheduling or processing methods to rest with small groups on the factory floor. If competition is based on flexibility to meet variable customer requirements, then a high degree of authority should be allocated to the workplace level. The interrelationship of these three organizational characteristics and their relationship to the orientations of first-line managers is shown in table 13. As in-

Table 13 Organizational characteristics and orientations of first-line management

Organizational Characteristics		Orientations	
		Supervisory	Managerial
Task structure	High		X
	Low	X	
Control system	Complex		X
	Simple	X	
Allocation of authority	High		X
	Low	X	

dicated previously, however, the factors influencing the nature of the control systems and the authority allocation within an organization are also related to the basic strategic position of the organization.[8]

Corporate Strategy and First-Line Management

The process of developing a corporate strategy is not always carried out in a carefully controlled and analytical fashion. A rapidly changing environment can result in corporate reactions which later become embodied in strategy. Societal expectations or relative competitive advantage can have either long-term or short-term influences on an organization's position. Corporate strategy is also influenced by the availability and nature of an organization's resources when compared with its competitors.

Historical influences may set the course of corporate strategy. An organization, for example, may have had a dominant strategic orientation towards certain markets, materials, or technologies which is difficult to change. Other factors that may influence strategy are the type of ownership, the relative dominance of particular suppliers, and the importance of particular customers.

Strategy should influence the competitive stance of an organization in the market place. Paul Marshall and his co-workers have categorized the basic competitive priorities of organizations as dependability, price or efficiency, quality, and flexibility.[9] An organization with an aggressive, thrusting image, for example, should be supported by operations that produce high volumes of relatively standard items by cost-effective methods. For manufacturers, the choice of a dominant competitive priority will influence the nature of their operations. A problem-solving type of organization, for example, is likely to have a job shop or a project type of production system. An organization that emphasizes low prices, however, is likely to use an assembly line or a job shop with large batch sizes. Manufacturing strategy should be formulated with regard to the appropriate competitive priority. As a result of strategy formulation, the detail of the manufacturing operation will emerge: the type of production system (continuous flow, assembly line, job shop, or project), the number of plants, the location and layout of each plant, the plant size or capacity, and labour force policies. The details of the operation will determine task structure at the workplace level, and the entire process will determine the type of control systems and authority allocation. As shown in figure 27, the appropriate role for the first-line manager should emerge as a result of considering all of the above factors.

It is not intended that the paradigm described above should provide a detailed organizational prescription but rather that it be used as a diagnostic tool. As noted previously, the first-line manager with a supervisory orientation is likely to be best suited to an organization in which there is a low level of task structure, a simple control system and a low level of decision-

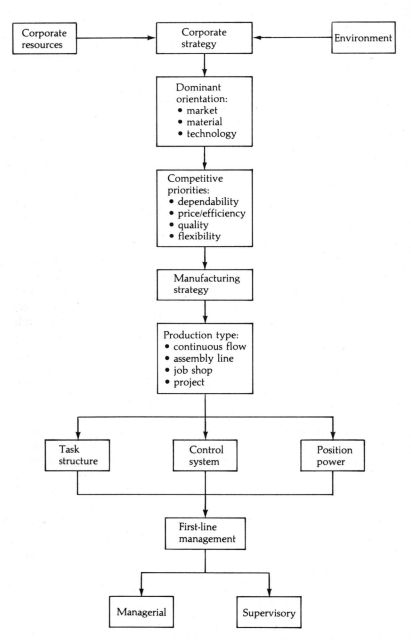

Figure 27 The effects of corporate strategy on first-line management

making authority. Concentration on output and efficiency by this type of manager is likely to be in line with the basic priorities of such an organization. By contrast, a managerial orientation is likely to be more appropriate in an organization where there is a high level of task structure, a complex control system, and a high level of decision-making authority.

The Production Process and First-Line Management

The dynamics described in figure 27 will not tend to operate unless some influence is exerted on the sub-processes involved. For example, cost effectiveness was the primary reason for the initial development of the assembly line type of production process. The entire production task was broken down into a series of very simple component tasks linked together serially. As the production process itself was so highly specified, the control system required was simple and the first-line manager had little relative authority. Hence, a supervisory style of first-line management was quite appropriate for an assembly line system of production. The task structure associated with a continuous flow production system is also relatively simple. The first-line manager is involved with routine monitoring tasks, and any serious abnormality in the system is dealt with by a technical specialist. The control system required is straightforward, and the authority of the first-line supervisor limited. As with the assembly line system, a supervisory style of management seems appropriate for continuous flow production systems.

Job shops differ significantly according to throughput volumes. A large job shop generates efficiencies from large production runs and few set-ups. Production planning and scheduling is not normally undertaken by the first-line manager. The tasks required of a first-line manager are relatively simple, and a supervisory orientation is likely to be quite appropriate. By contrast, a small job shop competes on the basis of flexibility and its ability to meet changes in customer demands. The first-line manager often plays a vital role in planning and scheduling production. As the tasks are complex and a high level of authority is required, a managerial style is therefore most appropriate. The project type of production process has similarities with the small job shop. Timing is of utmost importance, and often complex control systems are established to monitor a project. These characteristics require a more managerial approach or style at the first-line management level.

The influence of the production process on first-line management style is shown in table 14. It is important, however, to

Table 14   The normative effect of the type of production process on first-line management

Type of Process	Task Structure	Control System	Position Power	Style of First-Line Management
Continuous flow	Low	Simple	Low	Supervisory
Assembly line	Low	Simple	Low	Supervisory
Large job shop	Low	Simple	Low	Supervisory
Small job shop	High	Complex	High	Managerial
Project	High	Complex	High	Managerial

emphasize that the table shows a normative sequence of influences. Organizations can change components of this sequence successfully although it is sometimes difficult to do so. The Sidchrome divisions of Siddons Industries, for example, operates a large job shop. This would suggest that a supervisory orientation would be most appropriate. However, Siddons Industries has a policy of fostering employee participation in management decisions and is in the process of changing the task structure, control systems, and authority of the first-line managers to facilitate the development of appropriate styles.

Strategies for Changing the Role of the First-Line Manager

Two broad methods exist to improve the effectiveness of the first-line manager. The first method is to change the characteristics of the production process itself; the second is to change the work environment of the supervisor. In the context of the paradigm developed in this book, organizational change should involve an examination of the task structure, control system, and position power of the first-line managers themselves as well as those of other employees.

Traditionally, the supervisor has been regarded as the "boss of the shop floor". Increasingly, however, the supervisor is required to act less as a boss and more as a "resource person" to the work group for which he or she is responsible. In this role, the supervisor is now required to undertake a multiplicity of roles, which may include acting as a planner, provider, troubleshooter, and liaison person for the work group. For the most part, however, the supervisor is still in a transitionary stage somewhere along the continuum from boss to resource person. This has resulted in uncertainty and confusion for many supervisors, their work teams, and higher-level management.

The analysis of the changing role of the supervisor in various organizational situations has indicated that any new programmes of development and training need to take into account the following important factors:

Technological changes. In recent years, organizations have introduced increasingly complex and technologically sophisticated procedures. Advanced technology has been accompanied by a high degree of specialization, and the "traditional" supervisor often finds it difficult to cope with the new situation. Furthermore, the technical skills of many first-line managers are becoming outmoded.

Organizational changes. In the past, supervisors have often played an important role in decision-making at the plant level and have been the link between the plant manager and the shop-floor workers. Increasingly, however, the managerial hierarchy within many plants has become more extended and the supervisor has slipped several levels below the plant manager. A growing number of technical specialists and professionals have been added to the plant organization, and this has widened the gulf between the supervisor and the plant manager. As a consequence, first-line managers find themselves on the periphery of the decision-making process and feel displaced by middle management and technical specialists who have more direct access to the plant and influence on top management.

Changes at the workplace level. The traditional source of recruitment for first-line mangers was from the shop floor or workplace level. A person who performed well as an operator or tradesman could aspire to promotion into the supervisory ranks. The supervisor's authority was based on his or her experience and knowledge of activities at the workplace level which were gained over a period of many years. Social and technological changes, however, have transformed activities at this level so that they now bear little resemblance to the past. The shop-floor worker now often has a different ethnic background, sometimes has a higher level of formal education than the supervisor, undertakes more complex tasks, and has a different code of behaviour to his or her counterpart of the previous generation. Thus, there has developed an increasing gulf between shop-floor workers and their supervisors in terms of their backgrounds, qualifications, experience, and attitudes.

Changes in industrial relations. The pattern of industrial relations at the shop-floor level has undergone a number of changes, which has also affected the role of the first-line manager. The power and influence of shop stewards has increased, especially in the maintenance unions, while that of the supervisors has declined. Management have accorded greater recognition to shop stewards in negotiating changes at the plant level and have tended to use shop stewards as a communications link with the shop floor. The trade unions, for their part, are giving greater attention to the training of shop stewards in order to ensure that they are better informed and skilled in their role. By contrast, the training and development of first-line managers is often quite inadequate. There has also been a decline in the relative wages paid to supervisors compared with their subordinates, mainly as a result of pressure exerted upon employers by unions representing shop-floor workers. As a consequence of their perceived loss of economic status, power, and influence, supervisors have become increasingly unionized.

A Programme of Organizational Change Involving First-Line Managers

The following programme was undertaken within an

Australian manufacturing plant with the objective of improving employee relations and managerial effectiveness, especially at the level of the first-line manager. The programme originated from concerns expressed by the company about the poor performance of first-line managers in several of its plants. An investigation conducted by the company revealed the following problems:

1. Supervisors lacked commitment to company goals.
2. Supervisors did not identify with plant management.
3. Supervisors appeared, at times, to be hostile towards the company.
4. Many supervisors appeared to be demoralized and apathetic.

After considerable analysis of supervisory level problems in the organization, a number of contributing factors were identified. It was found that senior management, in general, had failed to recognize the important effects of social and technological changes on the role of the first-line manager. After discussions with consultants, the management decided that any programme that sought to change the role of the first-line manager in isolation from other employees was unlikely to be effective. It was therefore introduced to a programme involving representatives of all employees at one of its major plants. An assumption underlying the programme was that far-reaching social and technological changes were likely to occur within the industry in the years to come. In order to successfully adapt to future change, all employees would need to take stock of past experience and attempt to anticipate the future.

The Planning Workshop

A series of "planning workshops" were established with the assistance of consultants. The initial objective of the workshops was to review the strengths and weaknesses of plant operations during the past five years in order to plan more effectively for the future. The programme was based on the assumption that people would react positively to a genuine opportunity for involvement in decisions directly affecting them. The workshops would offer management and supervisors the opportunity to gain better insights into the views and aspirations of their employees. For their part, employees would gain a better appreciation of the way in which the enterprise operated as well as being able to present their views directly to management. The intention was not to supplant the established system of union-employer relations or to usurp the role of supervisors or middle management; rather, the workshops aimed to provide a supplementary channel for communications and broaden the decision-making process.

A series of workshops were held with four parallel groups: top management, middle management, supervisors, and shop-floor workers. Each group comprised approximately a dozen people who were drawn from a wide cross-section of the plant. The objective was to obtain groups that were broadly representative of the employees in the plant. The plant manager visited work groups throughout the plant and explained to them the nature and aims of the exercise. Each work group was asked to nominate or elect a representative to the workshop. The elected representatives were responsible for reporting back to their work groups on the results of the workshop at periodic intervals. Given the pyramidal structure of the organization, a smaller proportion of shop-floor workers were represented in the workshop than more senior levels. Nevertheless, the actual membership of the floor group was greater than each of the other three groups. Both the supervisors and middle management groups were drawn from all parts of the plant. The senior management group comprised representatives from both the plant and head office. This was in order to gain the perspectives of management from outside the plant on likely changes in the future, as well as provide the opportunity to inform head office representatives about the views of middle management, supervisors, and shop-floor workers in the plant.

The Workshop Programme

A series of phases were planned for the workshop whereby participants could gain initial acquaintanceship with others and develop working relationships which would assist them to collaborate more effectively in achieving the goals of the workshop programme. As shown in figure 28, five phases were planned over a nine-month period. Notices were placed on bulletin boards throughout the plant to inform all employees about the programme.

Phase 1. An initial half-day meeting was held with all participants in the workshop programme to explain the objectives of the project, to outline the methods that were to be followed in each workshop, and to provide a brief overview of changes that had occurred at the plant during the past five years since its establishment. Participants were also given the opportunity to question the plant manager and the consultants on all aspects of the proposed workshops.

Phase 2. A series of separate half-day workshops were conducted by the consultants with each of the four parallel groups: top management, middle management, supervisors, and shop-floor workers. The objective of holding separate meetings was to develop confidence and openness within each group so that they would be willing to share their views. The meetings were also used to review major changes in the plant during the past five years from the perspective of the members of each group. The consultants asked the participants to identify the strengths and weaknesses of the plant's operation during this period. Three aspects of the plant were explored: its technical efficiency, the relationships between employees and management, and the experience of individuals as members of the enterprise. These three dimensions were summarized as technical, social, and individual aspects of life in the plant. The participants in each group were asked to graph their experience on these three dimensions over the past five years. The results of each group were synthesized by the consultants and used for comparison in later discussions. During phase 2, each group was asked to nominate or elect representatives to form a composite group which would proceed further with the analysis of past performance and make recommendations to management concerning future plans.

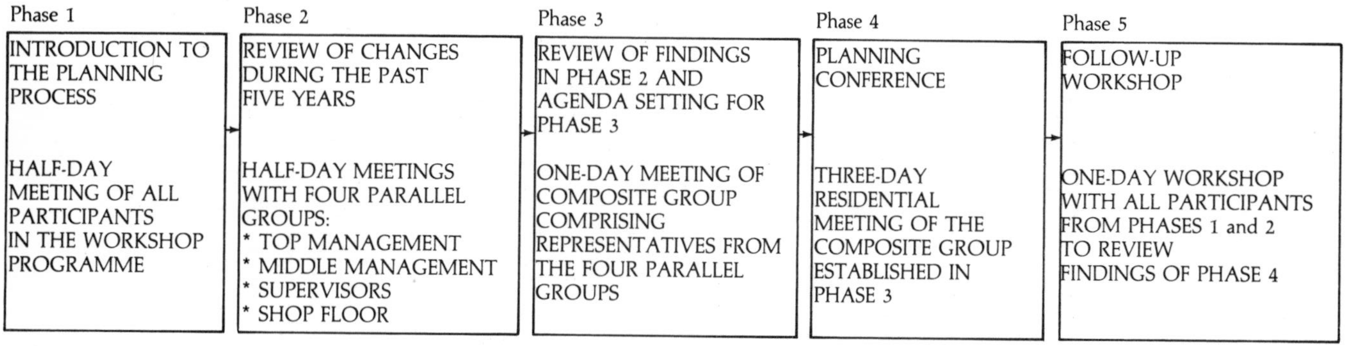

Phase 1	Phase 2	Phase 3	Phase 4	Phase 5
INTRODUCTION TO THE PLANNING PROCESS	REVIEW OF CHANGES DURING THE PAST FIVE YEARS	REVIEW OF FINDINGS IN PHASE 2 AND AGENDA SETTING FOR PHASE 3	PLANNING CONFERENCE	FOLLOW-UP WORKSHOP
HALF-DAY MEETING OF ALL PARTICIPANTS IN THE WORKSHOP PROGRAMME	HALF-DAY MEETINGS WITH FOUR PARALLEL GROUPS: * TOP MANAGEMENT * MIDDLE MANAGEMENT * SUPERVISORS * SHOP FLOOR	ONE-DAY MEETING OF COMPOSITE GROUP COMPRISING REPRESENTATIVES FROM THE FOUR PARALLEL GROUPS	THREE-DAY RESIDENTIAL MEETING OF THE COMPOSITE GROUP ESTABLISHED IN PHASE 3	ONE-DAY WORKSHOP WITH ALL PARTICIPANTS FROM PHASES 1 and 2 TO REVIEW FINDINGS OF PHASE 4

Figure 28 The workshop programme

Phase 3. A composite group comprising representatives from senior management, middle management, supervisors, and shop-floor workers met for a day with the consultants at an off-site location. The group spent the first part of the day analyzing the data yielded during phase 2. An important objective of phase 3 was also to enable the representatives from each group to get to know one another in preparation for phase 4. A subcommittee was established to plan the agenda for phase 4 based on the discussions during the day.

Phase 4. A three-day residential workshop was held away from the plant. This workshop represented the climax to the previous three phases which had provided the data to be discussed in phase 4. A range of problems which had been identified during the previous phases were analysed and a number of solutions were proposed. Top management also reported to the workshop on likely technological changes which would occur during the next five years and their implications for the plant. Although the workshop did not attempt to set out precise guidelines for the future, all participants were given the opportunity to make suggestions concerning long-term planning. The workshop also identified a number of problems which had occurred in the past and were of concern to employees in the plant. An important aspect of the workshop was the exploration of both differences and similarities in the views of employees at different levels and from various parts of the plant.

Six broad problem areas were identified during the workshop:
1. Communications, decision-making, and planning
2. Personnel matters
3. Safety
4. Technological change
5. Shift worker/day worker relationship
6. Other problems

Participants at the workshop worked in subgroups comprising representatives from all levels in the plant. A number of specific recommendations were made by each subgroup concerning each problem area.

Phase 5. A day-long meeting was held with all of the original participants from phase 1 of the programme in order to report on the outcomes of phases 3 and 4. All participants were given the opportunity to comment on the results of the three-day workshop. Top management also reported on action that had been taken on some recommendations and noted that consideration would be given to the feasibility of implementing other recommendations as a result of discussions during phase 5. A task force was established to further investigate problems that had been identified regarding the relationship between shift and day workers within the plant. It was also agreed that the plant manager would report back to the workshop at a future date regarding other recommendations which had emerged during phase four.

As shown in figure 29, the diagnostic model for organizational change emerged as a result of interaction between people in the workshops. What had initially started out as an elementary exploration of likely future social and technological changes that might occur in the plant became an exercise in organizational learning.

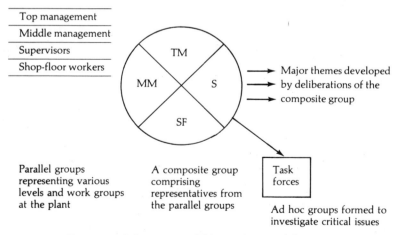

Figure 29   A diagnostic model for organizational change

Results of the Programme

As a result of the findings yielded by the workshop, the plant manager decided to appoint a programme co-ordinator who would assist management to meet commitments made to employees. A full-time training officer was also appointed to assist with the implementation of recommendations that involved the training and development of employees. An independent evaluation of the workshop programme was also undertaken.

The workshop programme was seen as successful in achieving its major objectives. Barriers between organizational levels were progressively removed, allowing for a full and open exchange of views. The spirit of co-operation generated by the workshop was regarded as valuable by all participants. The workshop facilitated consideration of the role of people in the plant, recognized the impact of technological change, and stimulated recommendations concerning action to be taken in the future.

Several limitations were seen, however, in the degree to which employees within the plant as a whole were able to be involved in the process. Those employees who participated in the workshop programme tended to be regarded as an elite by others. It was also felt that the workshop programme was regarded by many employees who were not involved in the process with a degree of cynicism or apathy. Concern was also expressed that the workshop might become a vehicle for the expression of industrial grievances which were more appropriately handled through traditional industrial relations channels.

The consultants had emphasized, initially, that the workshop programme should not be seen as a solution for all the problems faced by either the management or employees. The recommendations yielded by the workshop emphasized the necessity for gradual change in the organizational structure of the plant in order to provide greater flexibility and adaptation to change. Relationships between management and the unions were seen as being in "precarious equilibrium", requiring great sensitivity in the introduction of changes which might alter the relative strength of different groups in the plant. Nevertheless, the basic methodology used by the workshops which involved "vertical" and "horizontal" slices of the plant working on task-related problems was endorsed as a positive approach to introducing change.

Changes in the role of supervisory and middle management were seen as inevitable and possibly leading to conflict. The consultative approach which had been set in motion by the workshop programme, however, provided a useful model for the introduction of change. A prescriptive or unilateral approach by top management, in the face of the expectations generated by the workshop, would be likely to meet with resistance and be counter-productive. It was therefore decided to continue to work co-operatively with all levels in the plant, using the approach developed by the workshop programme, in order to assist people to adapt to change and enable a more flexible and long-term approach to be developed by management and employees within the plant.

Conclusion

There is no doubt that in coming decades the environment within which the Australian first-line manager works will continue to change.[10] Technology will continue to lessen the direct participation of labour in manufacturing processes as machine power continues to replace people. This process will either lessen the importance of the first-line managers or result in an expansion of their activities. First-line managers in the future will be more clearly designated for either a supervisory or a managerial role. Organizations will need to establish what is the appropriate role for their first-line managers and develop people accordingly. Unless the behaviour and objectives of the first-line manager are complementary to the competitive priorities and the corporate strategy of the employing organization, it will be very difficult to achieve operational objectives on the shop floor. In innovative situations, such as the establishment of semi-autonomous work groups or group technology cells, the formal role performed by a first-line manager as such may cease to exist. Acceptance of the new role of the "resource person" may require a detailed and clearly specified programme of change. Nevertheless, in most organizations, the first-line manager will continue to play a vital although changing role. The failure of Australian organizations to realize the importance of the various roles played by first-line management or to pay adequate attention to their interpersonal and technical needs will impede social and economic progress.

Notes

chapter 1

1. K.E. Thurley and H. Wirdenius, *Supervision: A Reappraisal* (London: Heinemann, 1975), p. 25.
2. *The Foreman: A Study of Supervision in British Industry* (London: National Institute of Industrial Psychology, 1951).
3. *Arbetsledarnas Rekrytering och Utbildning* (The Recruitment and Training of Supervisors) (Stockholm: Swedish Council for Personnel Administration and Swedish Supervisors Union, 1963).
4. Growing unionization among supervisors, however, may lead to a new sense of identity, as well as estrangement, from other levels of management.
5. Ministry of Labour, *The Training of Supervisors* (London: HMSO, 1954).
6. See, for example, F.J. Roethlisberger, "The Foreman: Man in the Middle", in *Human Relations in Administration*, ed. R. Dubin (Englewood Cliffs, NY: Prentice Hall, 1970), pp. 147-48.
7. S. Grabe and P. Silberer, *Selection and Training of Foremen in Europe* (Paris: European Productivity Agency, 1956).
8. See, for example, K.E. Thurley and A.C. Hamblin, *The Supervisor and His Job* (London: HMSO, 1963).
9. Thurley and Wirdenius, *Supervision*, p. 26.
10. G. Strauss, "The Changing Role of the Working Supervisor", *Journal of Business* (1957): 202-11.
11. See R.S. Fitton and A.P. Wadsworth, *The Strutts and the Arkwrights, 1958.1930: A Study of the Early Factory System* (Manchester: Manchester University Press, 1958).
12. See S. Pollard, *The Genesis of Modern Management* (London: Edward Arnold, 1965).
13. Quoted by R. Bendix, *Work and Authority in Industry* (New York: Wiley, 1956).
14. See A. Crichton, *Personnel Management in Context* (London: Batsford, 1968).
15. See K.E. Thurley, "Computers and Supervisors", *Productivity* 10, no. 1 (1969).
16. D. Nelson, *Managers and Workers* (Madison: University of Wisconsin Press, 1975), p. 34.
17. Thurley and Wirdenius, *Supervision*, pp. 211-14.
18. See P. Gilmour and R.D. Lansbury, "The Changing Role of the Supervisor: Im-

plications for Industrial Relations", *Journal of Industrial Relations* 19, no. 3 (1977): 225-40.

19. Thurley and Wirdenius, *Supervision*, pp. 223-24.

chapter 2

1. J. McIntosh, "Personnel Policies and Practices", in *Sources of Worker Dissatisfaction in Australia*, ed. R.D. Lansbury (Clayton, Vic.: Monash University, 1974), pp. 11-14.
2. R. Hurst, "Institutions, Processes and Objectives in Industrial Relations", in Lansbury, *Sources of Worker Dissatisfaction*, pp. 21-27.
3. K. Thurley and H. Wirdenius, *Supervision: A Reappraisal*, (London: Heinemann, 1973), p. 2.
4. See, for example, F.E. Emery, "The Assembly-Line: Its Logic and Our Future" in *Democracy in the Work Place*, ed. R.D. Lansbury (Melbourne: Longman Cheshire, 1980), pp. 197-205.
5. B.B. Gardner and W.F. Whyte, "The Man in the Middle: Position and Problem of the Foreman", *Applied Psychology* 4 (1945): 1-28.
6. F.J. Roethlisberger, "The Foreman: Master and Victim of Double Talk", *Harvard Business Review* 23 (1945): 285-94.
7. D.E. Wray, "Marginal Men of Industry: The Foreman", *American Journal of Sociology* 54 (1949): 298-301.
8. E.V. Schneider, *Industrial Sociology* (New York: McGraw-Hill, 1957), p. 143.
9. See R.D. Lansbury, "Specialists Versus Generalists in an Era of Change", *Journal of General Management* 3, no. 4 (1976): 55-61.
10. See R.D. Lansbury, "Professionalism and Unionization Among Management Service Specialists", *British Journal of Industrial Relations* 12, no. 2 (1974): 292-302.
11. Thurley and Wirdenius, *Supervision*, pp. 5-6.
12. H. Vander Hass, *The Enterprise in Transition* (London: Tavistock, 1967), p. 23.
13. D. Dunkerley, *The Foreman: Aspects of Task and Structure* (London: Routledge and Kegan Paul, 1975), p. 31.
14. See H. Peter, "Desigining Human Work: A New Challenge", *Work and People* 1, no. 1 (1975): 3-9.
15. T.U. Qvale, "What About the Foreman?", *Acta Sociologica* 19 (1976): 77-81.
16. P. Gilmour and R.D. Lansbury, "The Changing Role of the Supervisor: Implications for Industrial Relations", *Journal of Industrial Relations* 19, no. 3 (1977): 225-40.
17. P. Gilmour and R.D. Lansbury, *First-Line Management: A Study of Supervisory-Level Education in Australia* (Canberra: Technical and Further Education Council, 1977).
18. Australian Committee on Technical and Further Education, *TAFE in Australia: Report on Needs in Technical and Further Education* (Canberra: AGPS, 1974).
19. Australian Committee on Technical and Further Education, *TAFE in Australia: Second Report on Needs in Technical and Further Education* (Canberra: AGPS, 1975).
20. For an explanation of the statistical basis of cluster analysis, see G.H. Ball and D.J. Hall, *Background Information on Clustering Techniques* (Menlo Park, Cal.: Stanford Research Institute, 1968).
21. See K.E. Thurley and A.C. Hamblin, *The Supervisor and His Job* (London: HMSO, 1963).
22. The "human relations school" originated with the work of Elton Mayo and others at Harvard University in the 1930s, particularly in regard to the Hawthorne

studies. See F.J. Roethlisberger and W.J. Dickson, *Management and the Worker* (Cambridge, Mass.: Harvard University Press, 1949).

23. K. Lewin, R. Lippitt, and R.K. White, "Patterns of Aggressive Behaviour in Experimentally Created Social Climates", *Journal of Social Psychology* 10 (1939): 271-99.

24. R. Likert, *New Patterns of Management* (New York: McGraw-Hill, 1961).

25. D. McGregor, *The Human Side of Enterprise* (New York: McGraw-Hill, 1960).

26. F.E. Fiedler, *A Theory of Leadership Effectiveness* (New York: McGraw-Hill, 1967).

27. C. Sofer, *Men in Mid Career* (Cambridge: Cambridge University Press, 1970).

28. A.W. Gouldner, "Cosmopolitans and Locals: Towards an Analysis of Latent Social Roles", *Administrative Science Quarterly* 2 (1957): 281-306.

29. R.D. Lansbury, *Professionals and Management: A Study of Behaviour in Organizations* (St Lucia: University of Queensland Press, 1978).

30. R.N. Rapoport, *Mid-career Development* (London: Tavistock Press, 1970).

chapter 3

1. See, for example, G.D. Halsey, *Selecting and Developing First-Line Supervisors* (New York: Harper, 1955).

2. D. Roach, "Factor Analysis of Rated Supervisory Behaviour", *Personnel Psychology* 9 (1956): 487-98.

3. C.F. Dicken and J.D. Black, "Predictive Validity of Psychometric Evaluations of Supervisors", *Journal of Applied Psychology* 49 (1965): 34-47.

4. T. Burns and G.M. Stalker, *The Management of Innovation* (London: Tavistock, 1961).

5. E.L. Trist et. al., *Organizational Choice* (London: Tavistock, 1963).

6. J. Woodward, *Industrial Organization: Theory and Practice* (London: Oxford University Press, 1965).

7. C. Perrow, "A Framework for the Comparative Analysis of Organizations", *American Sociological Review* 32 (1967): 194-208.

8. K.E. Thurley and H. Wirdenius, *Supervision: A Reappraisal* (London: Heinemann, 1973), p. 109-12.

9. J.P. Meade and P.W. Greig, *Supervisory Training* (London: HMSO, 1966).

10. The human relations movement evolved from the work of Elton Mayo and other Harvard-based psychologists during the 1930s. It was later popularized in management literature by Douglas McGregor and others. See for example: D. McGregor, *The Human Side of Enterprise* (New York: McGraw-Hill, 1960).

11. P.B. Warr and M. Bird, "Assessing the Needs of Foremen", *Journal of Management Studies* 4 (1967): 332-53.

12. J.R. Armstrong, *Supervision Training* (London: Institute of Personnel Management, 1961).

13. Ibid.

14. See R.D. Lansbury, ed., *Performance Appraisal* (Melbourne: Macmillan, 1981).

15. Thurley and Wirdenius, *Supervision*, pp. 173-74.

16. Meade and Greig, *Supervisory Training*.

17. P. Hesseling, *Strategy of Evaluation Research* (Amsterdam: Van Goram, 1966).

18. Thurley and Wirdenius, *Supervision*, pp. 193-94.

19. Ibid.

20. See P. Gilmour and R.D. Lansbury, *Ticket to Nowhere: Education, Training and Work in Australia* (Ringwood, Vic.: Penguin, 1978).

chapter 4

1. D. McGregor, *The Human Side of the Enterprise* (New York: McGraw-Hill, 1960); *Leadership and Motivation* (Boston: MIT Press, 1966); and *The Professional Manager* (New York: McGraw-Hill, 1967).
2. R. Likert, *New Patterns of Management* (New York: McGraw-Hill, 1961); *The Human Organization: Its Management and Value* (New York: McGraw-Hill, 1967).
3. R. Smith, "Linked Work Groups Bridge the Communication Gap", *Work and People* 1, no. 2 (1975): 3-7.
4. Ibid.
5. See M. Rose, *Industrial Behaviour* (London: Allen Lane, 1975), pp. 188-94.

chapter 5

1. R.R. Blake and J.S. Mouton, *The Managerial Grid* (Houston: Gulf Publishing Company, 1964).
2. See H. Andreatta and B. Rumbold, *Organisation Development in Action* (Melbourne: Productivity Promotion Council of Australia, 1975), pp. 24-25.
3. Ibid., pp. 53-54.
4. M. Smith and C. Honour, "The Impact of Phase I Managerial Grid Training", *Journal of Management Studies* 6 (1969): 318-30.
5. See K. De Muse and S.J. Lebowitz, "An Empirical Analysis of Team Building Research", *Group and Organisational Studies* 6 (1981): 357-78.

chapter 6

1. D. Gerwin, "Do's and Don'ts of Computerized Manufacturing", *Harvard Business Review* 60, no. 2 (March-April 1982): 107.
2. G.A.B. Edwards, "Group Technology: A Technical Answer to a Social Problem?", *Personnel Management*, March 1974, pp. 35-39.
3. See R.C. Wilson and R.A. Henry, *Introduction to Group Technology in Manufacturing and Engineering* (Ann Arbor: Institute of Science and Technology, University of Michigan, 1977), chap. 2.
4. J.L. Burbidge, "Production Flow Analysis", *Institution of Production Engineers Journal* 42, no. 12 (December 1963).
5. L. Stiller, "Group Technology — Maximizing Its Benefits through Job Design", *Work and People* 7, no. 3 (1981): 24-55.
6. B.J. Dempster, Ajax Pumps; J.L. Burbidge, *The Introduction of Group Technology* (New York: Wiley, 1975); and C.C. Gallagher and W.A. Knight, *Group Technology* (London: Butterworth, 1973).
7. R.D. Pullen, "A Survey of Cellular Manufacturing Cells", *The Production Engineer*, September 1976, pp. 451-54.
8. See P. Noall, "Computer Aided Manufacture in Australia", in *Technological Change in Australia*, Report of the Committee of Inquiry into Technological Change in

Australia, vol. 4 (Canberra: AGPS, 1980), pp. 109-43; Gerwin, "Do's and Don'ts of Computerized Manufacturing"; and B. Gold, "CAM Sets New Rules for Production", *Harvard Business Review* 60, no. 6 (November-December 1982): 88-94.

chapter 7

1. T. Parsons, *The Social System* (New York: Free Press, 1951).
2. F.E. Emery and E. Trist, "Socio-technical Systems", in *System Thinking*, ed. F.E. Emery (Harmondsworth, Middx.: Penguin, 1981). See also E. Trist, *The Evolution of Socio-Technical Systems*, Occasional Paper No. 2, Ontario Quality of Working Life Centre, Toronto, 1981.
3. A.K. Rice, *Productivity and Social Organisation* (London: Tavistock, 1958), p. 4.
4. See R.D. Lansbury and G.J. Prideaux, *Job Design* (Canberra: AGPS, 1980), p. 12.
5. H.W. Peter, "Designing Human Work: A New Challenge", *Work and People* 1, no. 1 (Autumn 1975): 3-9.
6. See R.D. Lansbury and G.J. Prideaux, *Improving the Quality of Work Life* (Melbourne: Longman Cheshire, 1978).
7. A. Robinson and G. McCarroll, "A Work Group Approach at Welvic", *Work and People* 2, no. 2 (1976): 32-36, and A.R. Gibbons and G. McCarroll, "Welvic Revisited", *Work and People* 4, no. 1-2 (1978): 23-26.
8. R. Wild, "Job Restructuring and Work Organisation", *Management Decision* 12, no. 3 (1974): 121.
9. See J.D. Hill, W.A. Howard, and R.D. Lansbury, *Industrial Relations: An Australian Introduction* (Melbourne: Longman Cheshire, 1983).
10. M. Rose, *Industrial Behaviour: Theoretical Development Since Taylor* (London: Allen Lane, 1975), pp. 213-17.
11. A. Carey, "The Norwegian Experiments in Democracy at Work", *Australian and New Zealand Journal of Sociology* 15, no. 1 (1979): 14.
12. D. Silverman, *The Theory of Organizations* (London: Heinemann, 1970), p. 5.
13. J.E. Kelly, "A Reappraisal of Socio-technical Systems Theory", *Human Relations* 31, no. 12 (December 1978): 1069-100.
14. See F.E. Emery, "Semi-Autonomous Work Groups", in *Proceedings of the International Conference on Industrial Democracy*, ed. R. Wood (Sydney: CCH Australia Ltd, 1978), pp. 448-57; also F.E. Emery, "Designing Socio-Technical Systems for Greenfield Sites", *Journal of Occupational Behaviour* 1, no. 1 (1980): 19-27.
15. For further discussion of Woodlawn Mines, see G. Jackson, "Organization Development at Woodlawn", *Training and Development in Australia* 8, no. 4 (December 1981): 3-8.
16. P. Gyllenhammer, "Volvo's Projects in Human Engineering", in *Redundancy: The Post Industrial Change*, ed. G.W. Ford (Sydney: ANZAAS and John Wiley, 1973), pp. 75-78.
17. At the time of writing, 30 per cent of the operators in the mine are women, as are 10 per cent of the mill operators. There are no women employed as tradesmen in engineering. This percentage of women employed is the same as the ratio of female job applicants.
18. Marketing prepares an annual sales forecast from which the scheduling manager derives a three-month production calendar for each cell.

chapter 8

1. J. Child and B. Partridge, *Lost Managers: Supervisors in Industry and Society* (London: Cambridge University Press, 1982), pp. 214-15.
2. M. Maurice, A. Sorge, and M. Warner, "Societal Differences in Organising Manufacturing Units: A Comparison of France, West Germany and Great Britain", *Organization Studies* 1 (1980): 59-86.
3. Child and Partridge, *Lost Mangers*, p. 208.
4. E. Jaques, *A General Theory of Bureaucracy* (London: Heinemann, 1976).
5. J. Woodward, *Industrial Organization: Theory and Practice* (London: Oxford University Press, 1965).
6. W.A. Westley, *Quality of Working Life: The Role of the Supervisor* (Ottawa: Labour Canada, 1981), pp. 2-8.
7. For example, see L.W. Porter, E.E. Lawler, and J.R. Hackman, *Behavior in Organizations* (New York: McGraw-Hill, 1975), part 3.
8. For a more detailed development of the relationship of manufacturing and strategy see W. Skinner, "Manufacturing: Missing Link in Corporate Strategy", *Harvard Business Review*, May-June 1969, pp. 136-45, and S.C. Wheelwright, "Reflecting Corporate Strategy in Manufacturing Decisions", *Business Horizons*, February 1978, pp. 57-66.
9. P.W. Marshall, W.J. Abernathy, J.G. Miller, R.P. Olsen, R.S. Rosenbloom, and D.D. Wyckoff, *Operations Management* (Homewood, Ill.: R.D. Irwin, 1975).
10. D.C. Dunphy, *Organizational Change by Choice* (Sydney: McGraw-Hill, 1981), chap. 1.

Bibliography

Abhoud, M.J., and H. Richardson. "What Do Supervisors Want from Their Jobs?", *Personnel Journal*, June 1978.

Aguren, S., R. Mansson, and K. Karlssonn. *The Volvo Plant: The Impact of New Design on Work Organization.* Rationalisation Council, Sweden, SAF-LO, 1976.

Alderson, S. "The Jaquesian General Theory". In *The Glacier Project: Concepts and Critiques*, ed. J. Gray. London: Heinemann, 1976.

Alper, S.W. "The Dilemma of Lower Level Management: Freedom versus Control". *Personnel Journal* 53, no. 11 (1974).

Arbetsledarnas Rekrytering och Utbildning (The Recruitment and Training of Supervisors). Stockholm: Swedish Council for Personnel Administration and Swedish Supervisors Union, 1963.

Argyle, M., G. Gardner, and F. Cioffi. "Supervisory Methods Related to Productivity, Absenteeism and Labour Turnover". *Human Relations* 7 (1958): 23-40.

Armstrong, J.R. *Supervision Training.* London: Institute of Personnel Management, 1961.

Bailey, J.K. "The Essential Qualities of Good Supervision: A Case Study". *Personnel*, January 1956, pp. 311-26.

―――. "The Goals of Supervisory Training: A Study of Company Programs". *Personnel* 32 (1955): 152-55.

Bates, D., and D. Hosking. *Factors Which Influence the Success of Supervisory Training.* Engineering Industry Training Board, Occasional Paper no. 5, Watford, 1977.

Bedelan, A.G. "Superior-Subordinate Role Perception". *Personnel Administrator and Public Personnel Review* 15 (1972): 4-11.

Bedrosian, H. "Selecting Supervisors for Training: What Motivates the Boss?". *Personnel* 48, no. 1 (1971).

Berkwitt, G.J. "The Forgotten Front-Line Manager". *Management Review* 60, no. 10 (1971).

Betts, P.W. *Supervisory Studies*. 2nd ed. London: MacDonald & Evans, 1973.

Bittel, L. *Improving Supervisory Performance*. New York: McGraw-Hill, 1976.

Bittel, L.R., and J.E. Ramsay, "The Limited Traditional World of Supervisors". *Harvard Business Review* 60, no. 4 (1982): 26-36.

Blackler, F.H.M., and C.A. Brown. *Job Redesign and Management Control: Studies in British Leyland and Volvo*. Farnborough: Saxon House, 1978.

Bonham, T.V. "The Foreman in an Ambiguous Environment". *Personnel Journal* 50, no. 11 (1971): 841-45.

Bowey, A.M. "The Changing Status of the Supervisor". *British Journal of Industrial Relations* 11 (1973).

Boyd, B.B., and J.M. Jensen. "Perceptions of the First-Line Supervisor's Authority: A Study in Superior-Subordinate Communication". *Academy of Management Journal* 15 (1972): 331-42.

Boyd, B., and B. Scanlon. "Developing Tomorrow's Foremen". *Training Directors' Journal* 19 (1965): 44-45.

Braun, A. "Assessing Supervisory Training Needs and Evaluating Effectiveness". *Training and Development Journal*, February 1979, pp. 3-10.

Brianas, J.G. "Between Employees and Supervisors: Three Cases in Point". *Personnel Journal* 49 (1970): 892-99.

Brown, R.K., J.M. Kirkby, and K.F. Taylor. "The Employment of Married Women and the Supervisory Role". *British Journal of Industrial Relations* 11 (1964): 23-41.

Buchanan, P.C. "Evaluating the Results of Supervisory Training". *Personnel* 33 (1957): 362-70.

Buchanan, P.C., and C.K. Ferguson. "Changing Supervisory Practices through Training: A Case Study". *Personnel* 30 (1953): 218-30.

Burbidge, J.L. *The Introduction of Group Technology*. London: Heinemann, 1975.

Burns, T. and G.M. Stalker. *The Management of Innovation*. London: Tavistock, 1961.

Butler, W.P. "Job Satisfaction Among Foremen". *Personnel Practice Bulletin* 15, no. 1 (1959): 7-15.

Byham, W.C. "Changing Supervisory and Managerial Behaviour". *Training and Development Journal* 31, no. 4 (1977): 3-6.

Byham, W., and J. Robinson. "Interaction Modelling: A New Concept in Supervisory Training". *Training and Development Journal* 30, no. 2 (1976): 20-33.

Calhoon, R.P., and T.H. Jerdee, "First-Level Supervisory Training Needs and Organizational Development. *Public Personnel Management* 4, no. 3 (1975): 196-200.

Campbell, H. "Some Effects of Joint Consultation on the Status and Role of the Supervisors". *Occupational Psychology* 27 (1949): 200-206.

Child, J. "Factors Associated with the Managerial Rating of Supervisory Performance". *Journal of Management Studies* 17, no. 3 (1980): 275-302.

_____. "The Industrial Supervisor". In *People and Work*, ed. G. Esland, G. Salaman, and M.A. Speakman. Edinburgh: Holmes McDougall, 1975.

_____. "The Meaning and Process of Supervisory Unionism". University of Aston Management Centre Working Paper No. 172, February 1980.

Child, J., and B. Partridge. *Lost Managers: Supervisors in Industry and Society*. Cambridge: Cambridge University Press, 1982.

Child, J., S. Pearce, and L. King. "Class Perceptions and Social Identification of Industrial Supervisors". *Sociology* 14 (1980): 363-99.

Comptroller General of the United States. *Report to the Congress: Manufacturing Technology — A Changing Challenge to Improved Productivity*. Washington D.C.: U.S. General Accounting Office, 1976.

Cummings, P.W. "Measuring Supervisors' Responsibilities". *Training and Development Journal* 26 (1972): 24-27.

Dale, L.A. "The Foreman as a Manager". *Personnel* 48, no. 4 (1971).

Davis, D., and Z. Sabet-Shargi. "Development of Supervisory Performance Evaluation". *Personnel Journal* 50, no. 4 (1971).

Davis, L. "The Challenge for Production Management". *International Journal of Production Research* 9, no. 1 (1971): 65-82.

Davis, L.E., and E.S. Valfer. "Studies in Supervisory Job Design". *Human Relations* 19 (1966): 339-52.

Dickson, J.B. "Wanted: Professional Supervisors". *Personnel Journal* 52, no. 3 (1973).

Donnelly, J.F. "Participative Management at Work". *Harvard Business Review* 55, no. 1 (1977): 117-27.

Dowell, B.E., and K.N. Wexley. "Development of a Work Behaviour Taxonomy for First-Line Supervisors". *Journal of Applied Psychology* 63 (1978): 563-72.

Driscoll, J.W., D.J. Carroll, and T.A. Sprecher. "The First-Level Supervisor: Still the Man in the Middle". *Sloan Management Review*, Winter 1978.

Dunkerley, D. *The Foreman: Aspects of Task and Structure.* London: Routledge and Kegan Paul, 1975.

Dunphy, D.C. *Organisational Change by Choice.* Sydney: McGraw-Hill, 1981.

Eckles, R.W., R.L. Carmichael, and B.R. Sarchet. *Essentials of Management for First Line Supervision.* New York: Wiley, 1974.

Edwards, G.A.B. "Group Technology: A Technical Answer to a Social Problem?" *Personnel Management*, March 1974, pp. 35-39.

Emery, F.E. "The Assembly-Line: Its Logic and Our Future". In *Democracy in the Work Place*, ed. R.D. Lansbury. Melbourne: Longman Cheshire, 1980.

Emery, F. "The Fifth Wave? Embarking on the Next Forty years". *Human Futures and Public Enterprises*, Centre for Continuing Education, New Delhi, Winter 1978.

Fiedler, F.E. "Engineering the Job to Fit the Manager". *Harvard Business Review* 43, no. 5 (1965): 115-22.

Fleishman, E.A. "Leadership Climate, Human Relations Training and Supervisory Behaviour". *Personnel Psychology* 6 (1953): 205-22.

Fletcher, C. "Men in the Middle: A Reformulation of the Thesis". *Sociological Review* 17 (1968): 341-54.

The Foreman: A Study of Supervision in British Industry. London: National Institute of Industrial Psychology, 1951.

Fores, M., P. Lawrence, and A. Sorge. "Germany's Front-Line Force". *Management Today*, March 1978.

Front Line Management. London: British Institute of Management, 1976.

Fulmer, W.E. "The Making of a Supervisor". *Personnel Journal*, March 1977, pp. 140-43.

Gallagher, C.C., and W.A. Knight. *Group Technology.* London: Butterworth, 1973.

Ganzi, R.L. "Are Your Supervisors Earning Their Keep?" *Management Review* 60, no. 5 (1971).

Gardner, B.B., and W.F. Whyte. "The Man in the Middle: Position and Problem of the Foreman". *Applied Psychology* 4 (1945): 1-28.

Gelfand, L.I. "Communicate Through Your Supervisors". *Harvard Business Review* 48, no. 6 (1970): 101-4.

Gellerman, S.W. "Supervision: Substance and Style". *Harvard Business Review* 54, no. 2 (1976): 89-99.

Gerwin, D. "Do's and Don'ts of Computerized Manufacturing". *Harvard Business Review* 60, no. 2 (1982): 107-16.

Gilmour, P., and R.D. Lansbury. *Case Studies in First Line Management.* Canberra: Technical and Further Education Council, 1980.

―――. "The Changing Role of the Supervisor: Implications for Industrial Relations". *Journal of Industrial Relations* 19, no. 3 (1977): 225-40.

―――. *First Line Management: A Study of Supervisory-Level Education in Australia.* Canberra: Technical and Further Education Council, 1977.

―――. *Ticket to Nowhere: Education, Training and Work in Australia.* Ringwood, Vic.: Penguin, 1978.

―――. "Training First Line Managers for New Organizational Careers: An Australian Study". *Australian Journal of Management* 4, no. 1 (1979): 55-68.

Gold, B. "CAM Sets New Rules for Production". *Harvard Business Review* 60, no. 6 (1982): 88-94.

Goldstein, A.P., and M. Sorcher. *Changing Supervisor Behaviour.* New York: Pergamon Press, 1974.

Grabe, S., and P. Silberer. *Selection and Training of Foremen in Europe.* Paris: European Productivity Agency, 1956.

Griffin, R.W. "Supervisory Behaviour as a Source of Perceived Task Scope". *Journal of Occupational Psychology* 54 (1981): 175-82.

Guest, R.H. "Of Time and the Foreman". *Personnel* (1956): 478-86.

Halpern, R. "Employee Unionization and Foremen's Attitude", *Administrative Science Quarterly* 6 (1961): 73-88.

Hammer, T.H., and H.P. Dachler. "A Test of Some Assumptions Underlying the Path-Goal Model of Supervisor". *Organizational Behaviour and Human Performance* 14, no. 1 (1975): 60-75.

Halsey, C.D. *Selecting and Developing First Line Supervisors.* New York: Harper, 1955.

Hayes, R.H., and R.W. Schmenner. "How Should You Organize Manufacturing?" *Harvard Business Review* 56, no. 1 (1978): 105-18.

Hickson, D.J., D.S. Pugh, and D. Pheysey. "Operations Technology and Organization Structure: An Empirical Reappraisal". *Administrative Science Quarterly* 14 (1969): 378-97.

Hilgert, R.L., and J.R. Hundley. "Supervision: The Weak Link in Flexible Work Scheduling". *Personnel Administration* 20, no. 1 (1975): 24-26.

Hill, K. "The Selection and Training of Clerical Supervisors". *Personnel Practice Bulletin* 29, no. 2 (1973): 107-16.

Holt, H.F. "Problems of Supervisory Training: A Pilot Study". *Personnel Practice Bulletin* 14, no. 3 (1958): 7-14.

Hurley, W.M. "Supervisory Training at Nobel (Australia) Pty Ltd". *Personnel Practice Bulletin* 10, no. 2 (1954): 29-33.

Hutchinson, K. "The Selection and Training of Supervisors". *Personnel Practice Bulletin* 29, no. 1 (1973): 45-52.

Imberman, A.A. "Foreman Training: The Deal and the Reality". *Personnel Journal* 54, no. 4 (1975).

―――. "The Missing Element in Supervisory Training". *Management Review* 59, no. 3 (1970).

Imberman, W. "Don't Shoot the Foreman: Aim at the Plant Manager". *Atlanta Economic Review* 26, no. 1 (1976): 24-27.

Improving the Selection of Your First-Level Supervisors. Melbourne: Productivity Promotion Council of Australia, 1978.

Jenkins, C., and B. Sherman. *White-Collar Unionism: The Rebellious Salariat.* London: Routledge and Kegan Paul, 1979.

Jenkins, D. "The Supervisor Solution". *Management Today*, May 1978, pp. 74-7, 144, 147.

Johnson, G.R. "Supervision: A Two Way Street to Somewhere". *Personnel Journal* 50, no. 9 (1971).

Jones, L. "Improving Supervisory Performance". *Education and Training* 22, no. 10 (1980): 315-17.

Kanter, R.M. "Power Failure in Management Circuits". *Harvard Business Review* 57, no. 4 (1979).

Kavanagh, M.J. "Expected Supervisory Behaviour, Interpersonal Trust and Environmental Preferences: Some Relationships based on a Dyadic Model of Leadership". *Organizational Behaviour & Human Performance* 13, no. 1 (1975): 17-30.

Kay, B.R. "Prescription and Perception of the Supervisory Role". *Occupational Psychology* 37 (1963): 219-27.

Kirkpatrick, D.L. "Evaluating a Training Program for Supervisors and Foreman". *Personnel Administration* 14, no. 5 (1969).

Krackhardt, D. "Supervisory Behaviour and Employee Turnover — A Field Experiment". *Academy of Management Journal* 24, no. 2 (1981): 249-59.

Lansbury, R.D. *Professionals and Management: A Study of Behaviour in Organizations.* St Lucia: University of Queensland Press, 1978.

Lansbury, R.D. and R. Spillane. *Organizational Behaviour: The Australian Context.* Melbourne: Longman Cheshire, 1983.

Latham, G.P., and L.M. Saari. "Application of Social Learning Theory to Training Supervisors through Behaviour Modelling". *Journal of Applied Psychology* 64, no. 3 (1979): 239-46.

Latham, G.P., et al. "The Development of Behavioural Observation

Scales for Appraising the Performance of Foremen". *Personnel Psychology* 32 (1979): 299-311.

Lawrence, P. *Managers and Management in West Germany.* London: Croom Helm, 1980.

Lawrence, P.R., and J.W. Lorsch. *Organization and Environment.* Boston: Division of Research, Harvard Business School, 1967.

Lennerlof, L. *Supervision: Situation, Individual, Behaviour Effect.* Stockholm: Swedish Council for Personnel Administration, 1968.

————. *Dimensions of Supervision.* Stockholm: Swedish Council for Personnel Administration, 1966.

Lewis, B.D. "The Supervisor in 1975". *Personnel Journal* 52, no. 9 (1973).

Lull, R.A. "Clearing Away the Smokescreen Between Managers and Supervisors". *Management Review* 61, no. 9 (1972): 2-12.

McConnell, J.H. "The Assessment Centre: A Flexible Program for Supervisors". *Personnel* 48, no. 5 (1971).

McFillen, J.M., and J.R. New. "Situational Determinants of Supervisory Attributions and Behaviour". *Academy of Management Journal* 22, no. 4 (1979): 793-809.

Mann, F.C., and J.K. Dent. "The Supervisor: Member of Two Organizational Families". *Harvard Business Review* 32 (1954): 103-12.

Marshall, J.C. "Why Training for Supervisors?" *Training and Development in Australia* 1, no. 8 (1974): 18-19.

Maurer, J.G. "The Downward-Mobile Industrial Supervisor: Characteristics and Attitudes". *Sociology and Social Research* 53 (1969): 311-21.

Maurice, M., A. Sorge, and M. Warner. "Societal Differences in Organizing Manufacturing Units: A Comparison of France, West Germany and Great Britain". *Organization Studies* 1 (1980): 59-86.

Meade, J.P., and P.W. Greig. *Supervisory Training.* London: HMSO, 1966.

Meller, I.H. "The Effectiveness of Shop Stewards and Supervisors". *STUDIE* (Danish National Institute for Social Research, Copenhagen) 33 (1976): 121.

Melling, J. "Non-Commissioned Officers: British Employers and Their Supervisory Workers 1880–1920". *Social History* 5 (1980): 183-221.

Miles, R.H., and M.M. Petty. "Relationships between Role Clarity, Need for Clarity, and Job Tension and Satisfaction for Supervisory and Nonsupervisory Roles". *Academy of Management Journal* 18, no. 4 (1975): 877-83.

Ministry of Labour. *The Training of Supervisors*. London: HMSO, 1954.

Mitchell, T.R., and R.E. Wood. "Supervisors' Responses to Subordinate Poor Performance". *Organizational Behaviour and Human Performance*, 25, no. 1 (1980): 123-28.

Muendel, H.E. "Divisionalizing a Line Organization: A Challenge to the Traditional Foremen Training Concept". *Personnel Journal* 50, no. 1 (1971).

National Institute of Industrial Psychology. *The Foreman: A Study of Supervision in British Industry*. London: Staples, 1951.

———. *The Place of the Foreman in Management*. London: Staples, 1957.

Nealey, S.M., and F.E. Fiedler. "Leadership Functions of Middle Managers". *Psychological Bulletin* 76 (1968): 313-29.

Nelson, D. *Managers and Workers*. Madison: University of Wisconsin Press, 1975.

Newport, M.G., and W.J. Duncan. "Employees and Supervisors: Four Cases in Point". *Personnel Journal* 52, no. 7 (1973): 619-25.

Noall, P. "Computer Aided Manufacture in Australia". *Technological Change in Australia*. Report of the Committee of Inquiry into Technological Change in Australia, vol. 4. Canberra: AGPS, 1980.

Norton S.D., et al. "The Soundness of Supervisory Ratings as Predictors of Managerial Success". *Personnel Psychology* 33, no. 2 (1980): 377-88.

Oldham, G.R. "The Impact of Supervisory Characteristics on Goal Performance". *Academy of Management Journal* 18, no. 3 (1975): 461-75.

O'Reilly, A.P. "Skill Requirements: Supervisor — Subordinate Conflict". *Personnel Psychology* 26, no. 1 (1973): 75-80.

Page, M. "The Supervisor: An Endangered Species". *Works Management*, July 1977, pp. 74-76.

Paine, F.T., and M.J. Gannon. "Job Attitudes of Supervisors and Managers". *Personnel Psychology* 26 (1973): 521-29.

Partridge, B.E. "Influence and Responsibilities of First-Line Supervisors". University of Aston Management Centre Working Paper no. 129, February 1979.

Patchen, M. "Supervisory Methods and Group Performance Norms". *Administrative Science Quarterly*, December 1962, pp. 275-94.

Patten, T.H. "The Authority and Responsibilities of Supervisors in a Multi-Plant Firm". *Journal of Management Studies* 5 (1968): 61-82.

————. *The Foreman: Forgotten Man of Management*. New York: American Management Association, 1968.

Patton, J.A. "The Foreman: Most Misused Person in Industry". *Management Review* 63, no. 11 (1974): 40-42.

Penfield, R.V. "Identifying Effective Supervisors". *Personnel Journal* 50, (1971).

Pestonjee, D.M., and A.P. Singh. "Supervisory Orientation and Employee's Moral". *Journal of Occupational Psychology* 50 (1977): 35-91.

Petty, M.M. and G.K. Lee. "Moderating Effects of Sex of Supervisor and Subordinate on Relationships between Supervisory Behaviour and Subordinate Satisfaction". *Journal of Applied Psychology* 60, no. 5 (1975): 624-28.

Pfann, R.L. "Neither Fish Nor Fowl", *Personnel* Journal 54, no. 3 (1975).

Pfeffer, J., and G.R. Salancik. "Determinants of Supervisory Behaviour: A Role Set Analysis". *Human Relations* 28 (1975): 139-54.

Podsakoff, P.M. "Determinants of a Supervisor's Use of Rewards and Punishments: A Literature Review and Suggestions for Further Research". *Organizational Behaviour and Human Performance* 29 (1982): 28-83.

Porter, L.W., E.E. Lawler, and J.R. Hackman. *Behavior in Organizations*. New York: McGraw-Hill, 1975.

Production Promotion Council of Australia. *Survey of Supervisory Training*. Melbourne: PPCA, 1971.

Pullen, R.D. "A Survey of Cellular Manufacturing Cells". *The Production Engineer*, September 1976, pp. 451-54.

Qvale, T.U. "What About the Foreman?" *Acta Sociologica* 19 (1976): 77-81.

Reeves, E.T., and J.M. Jensen. "Public Seminars and Conferences for Supervisors". *Personnel Journal* 51, no. 5 (1972).

Roach, D.E. "Diagnostic Forced-Choice Scale for First-Line Supervisors". *Personnel Journal* 50, no. 3 (March 1971).

Roberts, B.C., R. Loveridge, and J. Gennard. *Reluctant Militants: A Study of Industrial Technicians*. London: Heinemann, 1972.

Roethlisberger, F.J. "The Foreman: Master and Victim of Double Talk", *Harvard Business Review* 43, no. 5 (1965): 22-52.

Roethlisberger, F.J., and W.J. Dickson. *Management and the Worker*. Cambridge: Harvard University Press, 1949.

Rosen, N. *Supervision: A Behavioural View*. Grid, Ohio, 1973.

Rosenbaum, B.L. "A New Approach to Changing Supervisory Behaviour". *Personnel* 52, no. 2 (1975).

Sasser, W.E., and F.S. Leonard. "Let First-Level Supervisors Do Their Job". *Harvard Business Review* 58, no. 2 (1980): 113-21.

Schappe, R.H. "The Production Foreman Today: His Needs and His Difficulties". *Personnel Journal* 51, no. 7 (1972).

Scheer, W.E. "A Practical Approach to Supervisory Training". *Personnel Journal* 48, no. 5 (1969): 369-71.

Scobel, D.N. "Doing Away with the Factory Blues". *Harvard Business Review* 53, no. 6 (1975): 132-42.

Siddons, J.R. "Industrial Democracy: Impossible Dream or Practical Reality?" *Australian Machinery and Production Engineering*, May 1977, pp. 30-32.

Simmons, R.G. "The Role Conflict of the First-Line Supervisor". *American Journal of Sociology* 73 (1967): 482-95.

Skinner, W. "Manufacturing: Missing Link in Corporate Strategy". *Harvard Business Review* 49, no. 3 (1969): 136-45.

Slusher, E.A., and P.A. Veglahn, "Retaining Minority Group Employees: Supervisory Training and Those Crucial First Impressions". *Personnel Journal* 51, no. 10 (1972).

Spencer, C. "The Personnel Problems of Medium and Small Firm". *Personnel Practice Bulletin* 26, no. 4 (1970): 255-29.

Spencer, C., and C. Singer. "The Personnel Function in the Medium and Small Firm". *Personnel Practice Bulletin* 26, no. 1 (1970).

Stiller, L. "Group Technology — Maximizing Its Benefit through Job Design". *Work and People* 7, no. 3 (1981): 19-28.

Strauss, G. "The Changing Role of the Working Supervisors". *Journal of Business* 30 (1957): 202-11.

————. *Improving the Quality of Work Life: Managerial Practices*. Springfield, Va.: U.S. Department of Labour, June 1975.

Strauss, G., and L.R. Sayles. *Personnel: The Human Problems of Management*, Englewood Cliffs, N.J.: Prentice-Hall, 1960.

Styles, P.L., et al. "Pre-Supervision Training at the George C. Marshall Space Flight Centre". *Personnel Journal* 51, no. 3 (1972): 190-98.

Sullivan, F.L. "Limiting Union Organizing Activity Through Supervisors". *Personnel*, July-August 1978, pp. 55-65.

Thurley, K.E. "Computers and Supervisors". *Productivity* 10, no. 1 (1969).

Thurley, K.E., and A.C. Hamblin. *The Supervisor and His Job*. London: HMSO, 1963.

Thurley, K.E., and H. Wirdenius. *Supervision: A Reappraisal*. London: Heinemann, 1973.

Toye, J. *Supervisors in Industry: A Survey of Research and Opinion*. Cambridge: Industrial Training Research Unit, 1978.

Truskie, S.D. "In-House Supervisory Training Programs: High Caliber, High Impact". *Personnel Journal* 58, no. 6 (1979): 371-73.

Van de Vliert, E. "Rose Conflict between Supervisor and Subordinate". *Personnel Review* 5, no. 1 (1976): 19-23.

Vecchio, R.P. "Situational and Behavioural Moderators of Subordinate Satisfaction with Supervision". *Human Relations* 34, no. 11 (1981): 947-63.

Wagner, L. "Leadership Style, Hierarchical Influence and Supervisory Role Obligations". *Administrative Science Quarterly*, March 1965, pp. 391-420.

Walker, C.R., R.H. Guest, and A.N. Turner. *The Foreman on the Assembly Line*. Cambridge: Harvard University Press, 1956.

Walton, R.E. "How To Counter Alienation in the Plant". *Harvard Business Review* 50, no. 6 (1972): 70-81.

Walton, R.E., and L.A. Schlesinger. "Do Supervisors Thrive in Participative Work Systems?" *Organizational Dynamics* 7, no. 3 (1976): 25-38.

Truskie, S.D. "In-House Supervisory Training Programs: High Caliber, High Impact". *Personnel Journal* 58, no. 6 (1979): 371-73.

Van de Vliert, E. "Rose Conflict between Supervisor and Subordinate". *Personnel Review* 5, no. 1 (1976): 19-23.

Vecchio, R.P. "Situational and Behavioural Moderators of Subordinate Satisfaction with Supervision". *Human Relations* 34, no. 11 (1981): 947-63.

Wagner, L. "Leadership Style, Hierarchical Influence and Supervisory Role Obligations". *Administrative Science Quarterly*, March 1965, pp. 391-420.

Walker, C.R., R.H. Guest, and A.N. Turner. *The Foreman on the Assembly Line*. Cambridge: Harvard University Press, 1956.

Walton, R.E. "How To Counter Alienation in the Plant". *Harvard Business Review* 50, no. 6 (1972): 70-81.

Walton, R.E., and L.A. Schlesinger. "Do Supervisors Thrive in Participative Work Systems?" *Organizational Dynamics* 7, no. 3 (1976): 25-38.

Warr, P.B., and M. Bird. "Assessing the Needs of Foremen". *Journal of Management Studies* 4 (1967): 332-53.

───────. *Identifying Supervisory Training Needs*. London: HMSO, 1968.

Warren, M.W. "Performance Management: A Substitute for Supervision". *Management Review* 61, no. 10 (1972).

Weed, S.E., T.R. Mitchell, and W. Moffitt. "Leadership Style, Subordinate Personality, and Task Types as Predictors of Performance and Satisfaction with Supervision". *Journal of Applied Psychology* 61 (1976): 58-67.

Weir, M., and S. Mills. "The Supervisor as a Change Catalyst". *Industrial Relations Journal*, Winter 1973, pp. 61-70.

Weiss, H.M. "Subordinate Imitation of Supervisor Behaviour: The Role of Modelling in Organizational Socialization". *Organizational Behaviour and Human Performance* 19 (1977): 89-105.

Wernimont, P.F. "What Supervisors Expect of Their Subordinates". *Personnel Journal* 50 (1971).

Westley, W.A. *Quality of Working Life: The Role of the Supervisor*. Ottawa: Labour Canada, 1981.

Wheelwright, S.C. "Reflecting Corporate Strategy in Manufacturing Decisions". *Business Horizons*, February 1978, pp. 57-66.

Wilson, R.C., and R.A. Henry, *Introduction to Group Technology in Manufacturing and Engineering*. Ann Arbor: Institute of Science and Technology, University of Michigan, 1977.

Wolz, W.T. "How to Interview Supervisory Candidates from the Ranks". *Personnel*, September . October 1980, pp. 31-39.

Woodward, J. *Industrial Organization: Theory and Practice*. London: Oxford University Press, 1965.

_____. *Management and Technology*. London: HMSO, 1968.

Wray, D.E. "Marginal Men of Industry: The Foreman". *American Journal of Sociology* 54 (1949): 298-301.

Yanouzas, J.N. "A Comparative Study of Work Organization and Supervisory Behaviour. *Human Organization* 23 (1964): 245-53.

Yuill, B. *Supervision: Principles and Techniques*. London: Allen & Unwin, 1968.

Zima, J.P. "Counselling Concepts for Supervirors". *Personnel Journal* 50, no. 6 (1971).

Index

Ajax Pumps, 81, 87, 88, 92, 93, 94
Amalgamated Metal, Foundry and
    Shipwrights' Union, 121
Amax Iron Ore Corporation, 72
Armstrong, J.R., 30, 31
Association of Drafting,
    Supervising and Technical
    Employees, 60
Australian Institute of Management,
    35
Australian Institute of Training and
    Development, 34
Australian manufacturing, 80
Australian Wire Industries, 67
Australian Workers' Union, 69, 121
authority allocation, 141-42, 143, 145
awards, 70, 72, 122

Bird, M., 30
Black, J.D., 26, 27
Blake, R.R., 64, 68
Broken Hill Proprietary Co. Ltd, 71,
    79
Burbidge, J.L., 81, 82, 83
Burns, T., 27

career orientation, 21-25, 137, 139-40,
    144-46
    cosmopolitan, 22
    local, 22
    managerial, 23-25, 137, 139-40,
        144-46
    supervisory, 23-25, 137, 139-40,
        144-46
career paths, 14, 21-25

Carey, A., 103
change programme, 148-56
Charity Organization Society, 7
Child, J., 133, 134, 137
collective bargaining, 108
Combined Union Committee, 70
communication, 50-51, 67, 74, 76,
    100, 121-22
computer-aided design, 89
computer-aided manufacture, 89
conflict, 52, 59, 69-71
contingency model, 19
control systems, 12, 112, 114, 141,
    143, 145
CSR Limited, 72

David Jones Limited, 49, 50
Dempster, B.J., 88, 93
Department of Labour, 13, 34
diagonal slice teams, 66, 78, 153, 156
Dickens, C.F., 26, 27
Dunkerley, D., 11, 25

Electrical Trades Union of Australia,
    121
Emery, F.E., 104

Fiedler, F.E., 19

Gallagher, C.C., 88
General Motors, 52, 53, 54
General Motors–Holden's, 59, 61, 62,
    63
Gilmour, P., 96

Goldsworthy Mining Limited, 69, 70, 72
Gouldner, A.W., 22
Grabe, S., 4
Greig, P.W., 29, 30, 32
group technology, 80, 81-83, 87-89, 141
  benefits, 86, 87, 92, 93-94
  machine layout, 81-82
  parts classification, 82-83, 87, 92
Gyllenhammer, P., 109

Hamersley Iron Pty Ltd, 69, 70, 72
Hawkes, R., 128, 129, 130
Hesseling, P., 33

KI Australia Ltd, 10, 101

industrial democracy, 12, 62, 125
industrial relations training, 78
Ingles, W., 91
Institute for Social Research, 43

Jacques, E., 135
job enlargement, 92, 94, 97, 111-12
job rotation, 111
job values, 116-17

Kangan Committee, 13
Kelly, J.E., 103
Knight, W.A., 88

Lansbury, R.D., 22, 96
leadership style, 43, 46
Lewin, K., 18
Likert, R., 18, 43, 44, 45, 46, 47, 48, 51, 52, 54
linked work groups, 47-52
Lippitt, R., 18

McGregor, D., 18, 19, 43, 51, 52
managerial behaviour, 64
managerial grid, 64, 65-68, 75, 76, 77, 123
managerial prerogative, 62, 134
manufacturing cells, 125-26, 128-30
Marshall, P.W., 143
Maurice, M., 134
Meade, J.P., 29, 30, 32
Meister, 133-34
Mitchell, C., 74

Mitsui and Co. Ltd, 72
Mount Newman Mining Company, 69, 71, 72, 74, 75, 77, 78, 79, 137
Mouton, J.S., 64, 68
multi-skilling, 104, 116, 119, 122, 124

National Institute of Industrial Psychology, 4
National Training Council, 34
Nelson, D., 7
Newman, I., 74
numerical control, 89

organizational context, 137-38
organizational development, 76
organizational goals, 61, 67
organizational strategy, 138, 142-45

Parsons, T., 95, 96
Partridge, B., 133, 134, 137
Perrow, C., 27, 28
Peter, H.W., 99, 100
plant design, 106, 108
process evaluation, 9
production systems, 138, 139, 140
Productivity Promotion Council of Australia, 34

quality of work life, 53, 61, 63, 112
Qvale, T.U., 12

Rapoport, R.N., 22
Rationalisation Council, 110, 113
Rice, A.K., 97
Roach, D., 26
role, 3, 7-8, 15-18, 30, 54-55, 59, 62-63, 77, 78-79, 86, 104, 108-9, 113-14, 123, 129-30, 138, 147-48, 156-67
Rose, M., 103

Stalker, G.M., 27
Stiller, L., 83, 84
Strauss, G., 5
self-managing group, 104
semi-autonomous work groups, 12, 98, 99, 100-101, 104, 108, 122, 123, 136, 137
Shell Company of Australia, 66
Siddons Industries, 105, 125, 146
Siddons, J., 125, 126, 128, 129

Silberer, P., 4
Silverman, D., 103
Sloan School of Management, 43
socio-technical system, 97, 104, 105
Sofer, C., 21
Sorge, A., 134
supervision:
    authority, 7
    definition, 4-5
    future, 8, 133-38
    systems, 6
    unionization, 8
supervisor:
    criticism, 10-11, 77
    career path, 21-25, 36-37
    education, 12-14, 25, 29-39
    effectiveness, 26-29, 142-45
    future role, 133-38
    role, 3, 7-8, 15-18, 54-55, 59, 62-63,
        77, 78-79, 86, 104, 108-9, 113-14,
        123, 129-30, 138, 147-48, 156-57
    style, 18-21
Swedish Council for Personal
    Administration, 4
systems theory, 95

task structure, 27, 86, 97-98, 101-2,
    112-13, 118, 141, 143, 145
Tavistock Institute of Human
    Resources, 96, 97, 98, 103, 104
Technical and Further Education, 12,
    35, 37, 39
technology, 27, 63, 79, 89, 97, 118,
    147
Theory X, 18, 19, 43
Theory Y, 18, 19, 43
Thurley, K.E., 4, 5, 6, 8, 9, 10, 11, 28,
    29, 31, 33, 38

"top-down" strategy, 61
Trades and Labour Council, 70
training, 29-39, 62-63, 66, 118-20,
    121, 123-24, 148, 155
    employee recognition, 35-37
    TAFE role, 37-39
training needs analysis, 119, 120, 122
Trist, E.L., 27

United Auto Workers Union, 53
utility trainers, 54

Van Etten, C., 90
Vehicle Builders Employees
    Federation, 10
Volvo Corporation, 58, 61, 104, 105,
    106, 107, 109, 110, 114

Warner, M., 134
Warr, P.B., 30
Western Australian Employers'
    Federation, 70
Western Australian Industrial
    Commission, 72, 73
Westley, W.A., 138, 139
White, R.K., 18
Wild, R., 102
Wirdenius, H., 4, 5, 6, 8, 9, 10, 11,
    28, 29, 31, 33, 38
Woodlawn Mines, 104, 114, 116, 117,
    118, 119, 120, 121, 122, 124, 137
Woodward, J., 27, 138
work group behaviour, 43, 46, 66, 86
worker participation, 12, 87, 97, 104
working ahead, 111, 112
works council, 108, 113, 125